Creative Skits

FOR YOUTH GROUPS

Randy Fishell
and
Greg Dunn

Illustrations by Ron Wheeler

BAKER BOOK HOUSE
Grand Rapids, Michigan 49516

To Tyler, a class act

—RSF

Acknowledgments

Here are a few special people who deserve a hand because they gave us one:

Jim Dunn
Garren Dent
Ted Hessel
Jon Anderson

And speaking of helping hands, Randy wishes to thank Diana, whose outstanding performance wins her the Best Supporting Wife Award.

Contents

Acknowledgments   7

Preface   9

1. The Supersaint Conversion Kit   11
2. The Great Pretender   19
3. Samaritan on the Silverton Trail   25
4. The Good News Investment Company   41
5. Under Construction in the Congo   49
6. Welcome Home   55
7. The Junkyard Jewel   65
8. Sinner's Point   69
9. Ticket to Heaven   79
10. What's Les Worth?   87
11. The Day the Mountain Moved   91
12. Something in Common   107

Preface

Clement Studebaker knew the time was ripe for change. As the president of a family-owned wagon and carriage building business, this astute entrepreneur realized that America was a nation on the move. Soon, this mobile society would require a more efficient mode of transportation. In 1897 Clement began experimenting with self-propelled vehicles.

Unfortunately he did not live to see his budding dream come to ultimate fruition. Clement Studebaker died in 1901. But by now his successor and former colleagues had seen enough to know that there was something to this horseless carriage idea. Combining superior craftsmanship with turn-of-the-century technology, a new kind of horsepower was hitched up to the front end of the Studebaker buggy. In 1904 the first Studebaker gasoline-powered car rolled out of the South Bend, Indiana, plant and into the annals of automobile history.

Although they were not the first gasoline engine vehicles to be marketed, those early Studebaker cars are today considered collector's items. But these automobiles represent more than just an unusual investment opportunity. They are the embodiment of what would eventually become an entire company's efforts to satisfy the needs of a new generation of travelers.

This book was written on a similar premise, one that suggests the need of adaptability in presenting the gospel message. Nowhere is this truer than in the area of ministering to today's youth. Communicating Jesus' eternal answers to youth's contemporary (and timeless) questions requires a new and creative approach. Christian drama provides such a vehicle.

Humorous at times, reflective at others, this collection of skits contains essential elements of many of Jesus' most significant teachings. Faith, humility, brotherly love, self-worth, and true spirituality are just a few of the areas touched on.

Written in a fun and easy-to-learn style, the skits can be used as either feature presentations or discussion starters. The props are simple, and a complete listing of the necessary items is included at the beginning of each script. The "Thought Starters" section is helpful in stimulating further consideration of a skit's theme. Also, the written introduction to each piece can be adapted to introduce the skit to your audience.

If your youth program is running smoothly, consider the lines on these pages a fresh addition to your arsenal of creative youth ministry material. But if you're stuck in a youth-group rut, it could be that it's time for a change. It is our hope that this volume will help to get things rolling again.

Randy Fishell
Greg Dunn

1
The Supersaint Conversion Kit

Characters

Ben Bogus, salesman

Bill Byers, prospective purchaser

Belinda Byers, his wife

Props

Suitcase

Christian literature

Flashlight

Small backpack (should be able to fit in the suitcase)

Gold-colored ruler

Contemporary Christian record album

Season pass to Noah's Ark Park

Bible

Sales-receipt book

Pen or pencil

Some money

Rotary Club pin

Cardtable

Have you noticed how many products have appeared on supermarket shelves lately packaged in plain black and white containers? Such items are called "generic," and they usually sell for much less than their colorful counterparts. We're led to believe that an attractive package means a superior product. But the fact is, it's what's inside that really counts.

Jesus once imparted a similar truth to a group of self-righteous Pharisees. The episode is recorded in Matthew 23:27, 28. Based on this incident, it seems clear that true Christianity involves more than appearances. And that's something you'll be sold on once you've seen Ben Bogus try to pitch his product: the Supersaint Conversion Kit.

Micah 6:8; Matthew 23:27, 28; John 4:23, 24

The skit opens with Belinda and Bill finishing their early-morning preparations for church (Belinda primping hair, Bill tightening his tie). They are standing in front of an imaginary mirror, facing the audience.

Belinda: *(Frustrated.)* Oh, I just can't get this hair of mine to do anything!

Bill: You've been using an awful lot of that French mousse lately. Maybe your hair can't understand English commands anymore.

Belinda: *(Sarcastically.)* Very funny. Well, this should hold through the pastor's sermon. *(Belinda begins to leave.)* You'd better hurry along, dear. It's almost time to leave for church.

Bill: I'll be right there.

(Belinda moves toward another area on stage. There is a knock on the door, and Belinda answers it.)

Belinda: Yes?

Ben: *(Dressed in a suit with bow tie.)* Mrs. Byers?

Belinda: Why, yes.

Ben: *(Steps in, speaks in fast-paced salesman style.)* Mrs. Byers, allow me to introduce myself. *(Shakes Belinda's hand.)* My name is Ben B. Bogus, and fortunately for you I have just the solution to your current perplexing dilemma.

Belinda: *(Confused.)* What dilemma?

Ben: Ah, ha! Just as I expected.

Belinda: What's just as you expected?

Ben: I expected to find yet more people whose situation was so serious that they themselves were unaware of their true condition.

Belinda: I'm still not sure what you're talking about.

Ben: I'm talking about the decided lack of conspicuous Christianity that permeates this town!

Belinda: *(Still confused.)* Would you excuse me for a moment? *(Steps back slightly.)* Oh, Bill, would you come here for a minute?

Bill: *(Walks over.)* Who's this guy?

Belinda: *(Pointing to Ben, but looking straight ahead.)* Take it.

Ben: *(Extends hand to Bill.)* Allow me to introduce myself. My name is Benjamin B. Bogus, and I have with me something no upstanding citizen of this community should be without.

Bill: Thanks, but we already have a vacuum cleaner.

Ben: A vacuum cleaner it isn't, but cleaning up your act is what my product is all about.

Bill: And what might that be?

Ben: *(Slaps the suitcase.)* I call it the "Supersaint Conversion Kit." If you have just a minute, I'd like to demonstrate how easy it can be to go from spiritual rags to heavenly riches.

Belinda: Well, we were just about to leave for church.

Ben: *(Assertive.)* I'm afraid church is just going to have to wait this morning. Step right this way and view my plan of transformation.

(Ben leads the Byers to a nearby area on stage. He places the suitcase on the cardtable and opens it.)

Now, Mrs. Byers, I can tell by the way you've readily welcomed me into your home that hospitality comes easily to you. *(Bill and Belinda look at each other.)* Because of that, I know you'll appreciate the first item contained here in the Supersaint Conversion Kit—*(Pulls out stack of literature.)* a six-week supply of four-color Christian literature. Place a few of these next to the cheese ball at your next party, and you'll send many a hungry sinner home with a bountiful supply of spiritual food.

Belinda: *(Somewhat impressed.)* They certainly look attractive.

(The literature is returned to the suitcase. The same should be done after each item is shown.)

Ben: *(To Bill.)* You, sir, on the other hand, appear to be the type of individual who might prefer a more direct approach to witnessing. Assuming I'm correct, *(Removes the flashlight from the suitcase.)* you'll enjoy this handsome flashlight made exclusively for this kit by the Laodicean Light Company. *(Turns flashlight on.)* Aim it out the window every now and again and your neighbors will know that you're doing your part to let your light shine.

Bill: What you've shown us so far does *appear* to have its benefits.

Ben: Believe me, appearances are what this kit is all about. *(Retrieves backpack.)* And to help foster the image you now know is needed, here's something both of you will find helpful. It's called the "Backpack of Burdens." *(Puts it partially on Bill, who buckles slightly under the weight.)* When your friends see you stooped over with this item affixed to your shoulders, they'll realize what a heavy load the true saint must bear.

Belinda: *(To Bill.)* This may be just what we need, honey.

Bill: *(Removing backpack.)* Well, a strong Christian platform could help my chances of getting elected to the city council.

Ben: Yes siree. And if there's a question in anyone's mind as to the sincerity of your beliefs, just furnish them this handy little gadget. *(Takes out the ruler.)* It's called the "Golden Ruler," and it rates your good deeds on a scale of one to twelve. One look at this unique device will be enough to convince any Doubting Thomas that when it comes to Christianity, you really measure up.

Belinda: *(Places ruler in Bill's pocket.)* Carrying that in your pocket really brings out the color in your Rotary Club pin, Bill.

Ben: Of course, how you look to your peers isn't the only thing that counts. It's also important to consider other individuals who may be sizing you up, such as our youth. And what better way could there be to help bridge the gap *(Brings out the record.)* than with this contemporary Christian record album. Just put it on the turntable and crank up the bass on the equalizer. It won't be long before today's kids realize they have a swell role model, worthy of their devotion.

Bill: I've always wanted young people to view me as someone they could look up to.

Ben: Well, with the sounds of Cross Elements [*May replace with another name.*] coming out of your speakers, the kids on your block will know beyond the shadow of a doubt that you're up to your ears in Christianity. Now, once you've gained a foothold with those same youngsters, they'll probably want to spend a lot more time with you. What environment could be more conducive to discipleship than a Christian theme park of world renown?

(Retrieves the pass to Noah's Ark Park.)

Here is a season's pass to Noah's Ark Park. *(Hands the pass to Belinda.)*

Belinda: *(Excited.)* Oh, that sounds like fun, sweetheart! Once the kids find out we've been on the Monkey's Tailspin, they're sure to think we're "groovy." *(Bill nods in agreement.)*

Ben: *(Grows serious.)* Now folks, I can easily see that you're an intelligent couple. But I'm sure that you would agree that in today's complex world, it takes more than brains to get where you want to go. Fortunately, you need not search any longer. Never again will your pious counterparts cast sidelong glances questioning your spiritual sincerity. Because now, *(Gestures toward suitcase.)* available to you at a bargain price of thirty-nine, ninety-five is a neat little package of religion so convenient you'll never want to leave home without it! So what do you say, folks, do we have a deal? *(Extends hand to shake on deal.)*

(Bill hesitates, peering suspiciously into the suitcase. A sly, confident grin then crosses his face.)

Bill: Well, not yet.

Belinda: Honey, you know what they say: "He who hesitates is lost."

Bill: That may be true in most cases, but not this one. You see, I happen to believe that our salesman is withholding one last item as a final incentive.

Ben: I'm afraid you're wrong. I've shown you the entire contents of the kit.

Bill: *(Reaches over and removes Bible.)* What's this, then?

Ben: *(Surprised, he takes the Bible from Bill.)* Huh, this Bible must have fallen off the dresser at the motel I stayed in last night. You're welcome to it if that will seal the deal. I'm not sure what you'd use it for, though.

Bill: *(Self-confident.)* We'll think of something. Throw in the Bible and you've got yourself a sale. But you'll have to write it up quickly or we'll be late for church.

(Ben returns the Bible to the suitcase. He then retrieves his sales-receipt book and speaks as he writes.)

Ben: Never let it be said that Ben Bogus was a stumbling block on the road to redemption. *(Hands receipt to Bill, who pays him.)* Thanks, folks. I'd love to stay and chat, but there are many others in this town who stand in dire need of conversion. Good day. *(Exits.)*

Belinda: Well, Bill, we'd better be on our way. Why don't you bring the kit along? I'm sure the pastor will appreciate our newfound sincerity.

Bill: Good idea, dear. *(Picks up Bible.)* Hmmm. I think we'd better leave this here. *(Hands Bible to Belinda.)* It's a fairly weighty book, and I'm sure this kit will be heavy enough without it. *(Closes suitcase as Belinda speaks.)*

Belinda: You know, I've always felt the coffee table in the den could use a little something more. This Bible is the perfect answer; it's just what we've been needing.

Bill: *(Ready to leave.)* Yes, that will look nice. But right now we're late for church. *(Picks up suitcase.)* Shall we go?

(Belinda sets the Bible down on the table as she begins to walk toward the door. She suddenly halts, looking first at the kit, then at her own clothes.)

Belinda: Oh, dear, this is awful!

Bill: What's the problem, sweetheart?

Belinda: I just noticed the color of our new kit.

Bill: Is there something wrong with it?

Belinda: Well, it's just that I'm a winter, and the kit is an autumn tone. I hate to say it, but I think you'd better go to church without me. I don't want anybody getting the idea that we aren't concerned with how we look.

Bill: Oh, I don't think you need to worry about that, dear.

Belinda: What makes you say that?

Bill: Because anybody with any intelligence knows that it's not what's on the outside that matters. It's what we have on the *inside (Gives the kit a gentle pat.)* that *really* counts.

**Thought Starters for
"The Supersaint Conversion Kit"**

1. What are the essential ingredients for true Christianity?
2. How does one obtain those important virtues?
3. Can you tell if a person is a genuine Christian? If so, how?
4. Is it all right to use Christianity as a "stepping-stone" to success?
5. Who comes to mind when you think of a true Christian? Why?

2
The Great Pretender

Achieving greatness is a goal many people strive for. Ironically, though, often those who try the hardest are those who fall the furthest short.

Not even Jesus' closest followers were immune to the desire for prominence. The Bible records in Matthew 18:1-5 one particular incident in which some of his disciples fell into a discussion about which of them would be the greatest in heaven. That's when they learned that Jesus' definition of greatness was far different from their own.

"The Great Pretender" will give your audience a ringside seat to take another look at some people's misdirected pursuit of greatness. We know you'll do just great, to say the very least!

Characters

Bubba Roper, prizefighter

Bam-Bam Mattson, title contender

Louie Cottrell, commentator

Spectator

Young boy

Referee (optional)

Props

2 sets of boxing attire, including gloves

Table

Chair

Microphone

Recording of crowd noise

A few sheets of paper for Louie (Can be script itself.)

Gym bag

Towel

White sheet

Overhead projector

These last two props are used to portray the fight scene in the following creative manner. First, a white sheet is suspended from the ceiling. (It's best if it reaches all the way to the floor.) Next, the overhead projector is placed behind the sheet, and aimed toward the audience. Just before the skit begins, the fighters (and referee, if used) step directly behind the sheet. When the overhead projector comes on, the fight is acted out in silhouette as Louie Cottrell comments. IMPORTANT: The boxers' movements should be timed to correctly correspond with Louie's commentary. That is, they should occur just *prior* to their being described.

Suggested Scripture

Genesis 11:1-9; Psalm 71:21; Matthew 18:1-5;
Luke 22:24-27

The skit begins with Louie doing a live play-by-play of the fight already in progress. Louie should speak in a manner similar to that of sportscaster Howard Cosell. The spectator can be sitting in the front row of the audience. A tape of crowd noise should be playing in the background.

Cottrell: *(Excitedly.)* The champ is in his usual fine form today. He's kept Mattson in a defensive posture for most of the fight so far. *(Loudly.)* And there's an uppercut to Mattson's jaw! He's hurting, and now he begins to reel! Roper moves in for the kill. He circles Mattson, taunting the woozy challenger. I've seen a lot of great fighters through the years, but Roper's proving again today why he's the best ever. We're only in the third round, but it looks like Mattson won't be able to stay on his feet much longer. *(More excitedly.)* And there it is! Roper delivers a blow to the face! Bam-Bam Mattson is down. Roper lifts his arms in triumph, and the count begins. Ten, nine—the Champ now points and jeers at his prone opponent. Eight, seven, six— *(Almost shouting.)* Mattson's trying to get up, he pulls himself up on his elbows. He hesitates, but now he's down again! The count continues—five, four—Roper begins prancing about in his corner, shouting, "I'm the greatest!" And indeed he *is* the greatest! Two, one, the count is over, and the Champ has done it again! Maybe we can get a few words from Bubba. *(To Bubba.)* Champ, can we see you over here for a quick interview?

(Bubba moves toward Louie, while the other fighter exits offstage. The spectator now drifts over near the interview to take in the conversation. The crowd noise fades out.)

Bubba: *(Slightly out of breath, towel around neck.)* What's up, Louie?

Louie: Champ, it's not what's up but rather who's down, and that's Bam-Bam Mattson!

Bubba: *(Exhibiting extreme self-confidence.)* I don't really think that comes as a surprise to anybody. And if there *was* a question in anyone's mind as to who's the greatest, tonight's performance should put an end to that doubt. *(Lifts arms.)*

Louie: And an impressive display it was, Bubba. Tell me, is there one factor more than any other that has proved to be a major ingredient in your boxing success?

Bubba: Without question, Louie. You're only going to be as good as you think you are. Early in my career I learned that if you want to be *good*, then that's all you'll ever be—you'll never be *great*. That's the difference between me and the others. They may be good, but *(Shouts.)* I'm the greatest!

Louie: Well, you've definitely made it clear tonight that you pack a powerful punch that few people have enough luck to duck! Champ, thanks so much for your time. I won't keep you any longer as you're undoubtedly wanting to get down to the hotel for the official presentation of the championship trophy. And with that, ladies and gentlemen, I'm going to duck out of here. I hope you've enjoyed tonight's fight. Until next time, this is Louie Cottrell going out like a light.

(Louie quickly collects his gear, except for a few sheets of paper, then exits. At the same time, Bubba heads the opposite direction toward the locker room. A tap on the shoulder from the spectator stops him.)

Bubba: *(Turns toward spectator.)* What do you want?

Spectator: I'm curious about something. Are you really as arrogant as you seem, or is it just an act you're putting on?

Bubba: *(Taken aback.)* What are you talking about?

Spectator: I'm referring to your claims about being the "greatest." Do you really think that just because you have the ability to consistently knock people out, you're somehow superior to the rest of us?

Bubba: Maybe you'd like to find out for yourself, Noodle Dukes.

Spectator: I don't doubt that you could give me a quick facelift. But laying me out flat would only confirm my suspicion that your so-called "greatness" comes from the hand, and not from the heart. Frankly, I didn't come here tonight to see who would knock out who. I came to discover whether you were really a champion— or just a "great" pretender. I think I have a clearer picture now which of those you really are.

(The spectator turns and exits. Bubba reflects momentarily on the encounter, then turns and walks toward the locker room once more. As his hand reaches out to open the door, he hears a whimpering sound. Turning around, he sees a young boy walking aimlessly and wiping tears from his eyes. Bubba turns back to enter the locker room, and then pauses briefly with his hand on the doorknob. He then looks at the boy again and walks over to him.)

Bubba: *(Awkwardly.)* What's the matter, kid?

Boy: *(Lifts his head and sees the Champ.)* You, you're Bubba Roper! You're the greatest, Champ!

Bubba: Yeah, that's right. So what's wrong?

Boy: Nothin'.

Bubba: It looks like you've been crying. *(Takes towel from around neck and hands it to boy.)* Here, use this.

Boy: *(Embarrassed.)* I wasn't really crying. *(Wipes eyes and cheeks.)* I just got somethin' in my eye.

Bubba: This may surprise you, kid, but when I was your age I used to get those same things in my eyes sometimes. They're called tears. Now, what've you been crying about?

Boy: (*Still sniffling.*) Well, I came here with my older brother and some of his friends. But they must've forgotten about me, 'cause they left me here all alone with no way to get home.

Bubba: Where do you live?

Boy: Fifty-ninth and Grant.

Bubba: That's clear on the other side of the city! Can't you call your parents?

Boy: We don't have a phone. Besides, my mom works at night.

Bubba: (*After slight hesitation.*) Well, it looks like you're in a real jam. I hope you get yourself out of it.

(*Bubba walks away and enters the locker room. The boy continues walking slowly, and wipes his cheeks again. After a brief pause, Bubba, carrying his gym bag, reenters and walks slowly over toward the boy. At the same time, Louie Cottrell returns to collect his forgotten papers.*)

Louie: (*Surprised.*) Why, Champ! I thought you'd be on your way to the hotel by now. If it's a ride you're in need of, allow me to offer my services.

Bubba: No, thanks, Louie. I've got something, I mean, (*Looks at boy.*) some*one* to take care of first. (*Puts arm around boy.*) Come on kid. My car's out back. I can give you a lift home.

Louie: (*Concerned.*) Hmmm. If you don't mind my saying so, Champ, making the crowd wait while you take this kid home—well, let's just say the idea doesn't sound too great.

Bubba: It may not seem too great, Louie, but one thing's sure.

Louie: What's that?

Bubba: (*Stops.*) It's the best move I've made in a long time.

(*Bubba and boy exit. Louie leaves in opposite direction.*)

Thought Starters for "The Great Pretender"

1. What makes a person "great"?
2. Should an individual avoid striving for earthly greatness?

3. Why do most people seem to want to "be somebody"?
4. Who is the greatest person you have ever met?
5. How can a person be assured of achieving true greatness?

3

Samaritan on the Silverton Trail

Characters

Bill Connors, sheriff

John Slade, banker

Lucille Perkins, hotel owner

Joe Krebs, cowhand

Eustace, prospector

Joshua Gilbert, preacher

Reginald Pittman, railroad
   magnate

Frank Littleton, piano player

Props

Appropriate western attire for
   each character

Badge, gun with holster (for
   Connors)

Horse brush (for Krebs)

Tin pan (for Eustace)

Paper (or blueprint, for Pittman)

Old-fashioned raincoat. The coat
   must have a bit of adobe-
   colored mud purposely placed

The question posed to Jesus by the "expert in the law" was straightforward. He simply wanted to know, "What must I do to inherit eternal life?" Jesus explained that the two basic requirements were to love God and our neighbor. But the lawyer appeared to still be confused. He then asked another question. "And who is my neighbor?" Then followed what has become one of Jesus' most-loved narratives, the story of the good Samaritan. You'll find it in Luke 10:25–37.

Here's a unique approach to the message contained in the good Samaritan story. This play carries a western theme, and is performed in the style of the classic mystery adventure known as the "whodunit." But your audience won't be trying to expose the doer of a dastardly deed. Instead, they'll be attempting to discover the true identity of the person who dared enough to care. Enjoy your journey as you travel down the Silverton Trail!

on its tail. This can be made from water, flour, and food coloring if necessary.

Old-fashioned coatrack

2 chairs

Optional: bandage (for Slade)

Suggested Scripture

Mark 12:28-34; Luke 6:31, 10:25-37; 1 John 4:19-21

The skit opens with the characters located at various points on stage. They should remain in a "freeze" position until Connors steps over to interview them. The coatrack should be placed near Pittman. The muddied coat is hung on it, with the tail partially exposed to the audience. Western piano music begins in the background. Connors enters and directs his opening remarks toward the audience.

Connors: The American frontier. It's an untamed land, filled with hired hands and gambling gunmen. But it's also a place where anyone willing to work up a sweat can stake a claim on the future. Some do it the honest way; others simply take what they can get, however they can get it. Fortunately, there's an occasional person who tries to make up for the underhanded types. I'd like to tell you about one of those folk.

It happened a couple of years ago. One night our banker here in Eureka, John Slade, got himself held up out on the Silverton Trail. *(Slade, sitting down, "unfreezes" and begins rubbing the back of his head.)* The bandit took all his money and left him with nothing but a knot on his head. But there was something even more puzzling than who robbed the banker. The *real* mystery was who brought the unconscious Slade back to town.

(Connors walks over and sits down in a chair next to Mr. Slade.)

Slade: *(Irritated.)* Sheriff, if my head didn't hurt so bad I'd tell you exactly what I think of the law enforcement around here.

Connors: I'm sorry for the trouble you ran into, Mr. Slade. I'd appreciate it if you'd tell me exactly what happened.

Slade: Not that I think it will do any good, but here's what I remember. I was down in Silverton appraising land for some clients. I finished up my business late last night. Then I mounted up for the fifteen-mile ride back to Eureka. As best as I can tell, I was coming around Adobe Bend, about halfway between Silverton and Eureka, when it happened. It was a little hard to see because it was dark and rainy. Suddenly someone jumped out from behind a boulder, waved a shotgun in my face and ordered me off my horse. Then I felt a sharp pain in the back of my head. The next thing I knew the doc was working on me in the lobby of the Grant Hotel.

Connors: Doc tells me you were mighty lucky. Whoever brought you into town bandaged your head. He says you could've bled to death if it weren't for that person.

Slade: I'll have to admit I'm indebted to that individual.

Connors: Is there anything else you remember about the incident?

Slade: Well, now that you mention it, there was one other thing. I must've gotten hit pretty hard, because for a minute I thought I was headed for the pearly gates. As I was lying there beside the road, I was sure somebody nearby was singing "Bringing in the Sheaves." Funny what kind of tricks a person's half-conscious mind will play on him, isn't it sheriff?

Connors: It *is* a might unusual, Mr. Slade. But I'm still curious to know who it was that brought you back into town.

Slade: I wish I could tell you. But, frankly, I don't have the slightest idea who that person might have been.

Connors: Well, Mr. Slade, that's precisely what I intend to find out.

(*Short piano interlude. Slade nods good-bye and exits. Connors walks the opposite direction and continues his narration.*)

(*Narrating to audience while approaching Lucille Perkins.*) I knew that discovering the identity of Mr. Slade's benefactor would be a tough task. (*Lucille, with back toward audience begins the motions of placing mail in the mailslots behind the counter.*) But the logical place to start was close at hand. I walked over to the Grant Hotel, where Lucille Perkins was working at the desk.

(*Connors clears his throat. Lucille whirls around and speaks to him.*)

Lucille: Good morning, sheriff! Is it clearing up outside yet? That was quite a storm we had last night. *(Connors nods.)* Speaking of last night, have you found the man who robbed Mr. Slade?

Connors: No, not yet.

Lucille: And to think I was on that very road yesterday myself. I shudder to think what might have happened.

Connors: Well, don't you worry too much about it, Miss Perkins. I'm sure the lawbreaker will be brought to justice. Right now, though, my interest lies elsewhere. You mentioned *you* were on the Silverton Trail yesterday.

Lucille: As a matter of fact, I was, sheriff. Mrs. Colby's been under the weather all week so I thought she'd enjoy a bowl of hot soup. I sat a spell with her, but I had to get back to the hotel for supper. Short as it was, I think Mrs. Colby enjoyed the visit.

Connors: That's mighty kind of you. I can't think of anyone on the whole western slope who has a bigger heart than you do, Miss Perkins.

Lucille: Why, thank you, sheriff. Now, if you'll excuse me, I'd better check and see how the noon meal is coming along.

(Connors tips hat, Lucille exits. The sheriff then narrates as he moves toward Joe Krebs.)

Connors: I left the Grant Hotel having learned some significant facts—but I knew I didn't have the complete picture yet. I made my way down the street and, as luck would have it, spotted another potential source of information near the livery stable. *(Joe begins motion of brushing his horse.)* Joe Krebs was a cowhand over at the Circle V ranch. I knew Joe had taken a fancy to Mr. Slade's daughter, Daisy Mae. Hoping to discover what Joe knew about last night's events, I crossed the street and greeted him. It wasn't long before the conversation got around to Mr. Slade.

(Krebs speaks to Connors while he continues to brush his horse.)

Krebs: It's enough to make even myself a might uncomfortable, sheriff. Not that I'm a yellow belly or anything. But just the same, next time I'm on the Silverton Trail I'm gonna make sure I got somethin' besides a pocket hangin' on the side of my leg.

Connors: Well, now, Joe, I don't think there's any reason to get an itchy trigger finger over this thing. Sooner or later, we'll find the guilty person. By the way, how's Daisy Mae these days?

Krebs: *(Stops brushing horse.)* Now if that don't beat all. How'd you find out about me and Daisy Mae?

Connors: *(Smiling.)* It's pretty hard to keep a thing like that a secret. I'll say one thing—she's a mighty fine lookin' young lady. Any thoughts of marriage?

Krebs: *(Sheepishly.)* Well, as a matter of fact, yes. *(Joe leans in closer to the sheriff.)* Just between you and me, I brought up the subject to Daisy Mae last night. I didn't exactly mean to. It just sorta happened. We was out walkin' under the stars, and I guess they kinda lent themselves to talkin' about love. Yes, sir, if it was up to the two of us, we'd get ourselves hitched tomorrow!

Connors: *Isn't* it up to the two of you?

Krebs: Ha! I ain't seen a member of the Slade family yet who's been able to make a decision without the old man interferin'. That's especially true when it comes to one of his daughters gettin' married. Seems he thinks a cowhand ain't quite good enough for one of his little girls.

Connors: Has he ever told you that?

Krebs: That old critter don't need to *say* anything. I can tell he don't like me just by the way his eyeballs get narrow every time he sees me. Besides, Daisy Mae knows it's true. Just last night she told me that next to Reginald Pittman, I'm the topic of more ill conversation around their house than anyone else. That made me so mad I up and left her standin' alone on the porch. I just wasn't thinkin' straight. I decided to go for a ride in the moonlight to cool off. I'll tell you one thing—I felt a whole lot better when I got back.

Connors: You say you went for a ride last night. Which direction did you go?

Krebs: I headed south, on the Silverton Trail.

Connors: *(Pauses.)* It's been nice chattin' with you, Joe.

(Piano bridge, Joe nods and leads his horse offstage. Connors then resumes narration while strolling toward the next character.)

Joe Krebs had left me considerably more enlightened as to the likelihood of *his* being Mr. Slade's "good Samaritan." As I pondered Joe's remarks, I heard clanking sounds coming from down the street. *(Eustace enters from rear of audience. He is accompanied by an imaginary mule.)* It was a prospector with his mule. I struck up a conversation with the crusty old man. It turned out his name was Eustace, and he had been panning for gold in the San Juan mountains. After buying a few supplies, he was headed north.

Eustace: *(With appropriate inflections.)* Yes siree, a prospector's life ain't easy. Between restockin' my pack and my empty belly, I figure I'll 'bout have spent my last dollar. Got to admit, though, them was some mighty fine vittles I had down at that there Grant Hotel this mornin.'

Connors: Oh, you've been in town all day?

Eustace: Got in last night. Hitched Stubby here up to a post and spread my blanket out in the livery stable.

Connors: Eustace, have you ever been in our town before?

Eustace: Once. Came to see a man named Slade. Figured a small-town banker might be willin' to stake grub on my prospectin' operation. No luck though. I might just as well been talkin' finances to my mule!

Connors: I see. I guess if you came from the San Juans, you must've come in on the Silverton Trail.

Eustace: That's the only way I know of that a fella kin get from there ta here. And speakin' of the Silverton Trail, you don't happen to know of anybody around these parts who rides a big Palomino, do ya? If ya does, I'd be mighty obliged if you'd give him a piece of my mind. That buzzard passed me out there near Adobe Bend last night ridin' like the wind. Kicked up so much dust, I almost choked ta death!

Connors: As a matter of fact, I *do* happen to know someone who owns a large Palomino. I may even have reason to see him soon.

Eustace: Well, when ya does, tell him he orrta learn how to ride a little more gentlemanlike! I don't like to take a bath any more often than I hafta!

(Upbeat piano bridge. Eustace exits. Connors begins narrating again while walking.)

Eustace had been very informative. His remarks had brought to mind Mr. Reginald Pittman, owner of one of the finest Palomino horses on the western slope. He was also the sole proprietor of the only railway system in the territory. Some people felt he'd taken advantage of a number of the local ranchers in acquiring their land to lay his track on. Business dealings aside, though, I decided to pay Mr. Pittman a visit.

(Here, soft religious music should begin playing in the background. A real organ is best, but a piano is also suitable.)

Before I got to his place just north of town, however, I happened to catch some strains of music coming from the town church. I had heard that on occasion Reverend Gilbert had assisted those in need. Considering the nature of my current investigation, it seemed logical that he should be considered a suspect as the possible "Samaritan." I entered the church, pausing to listen for a moment to the music.

(Connors slowly opens the church door, removes his hat and stands reverently listening to the music. Shortly, Reverend Gilbert approaches from Connors' blind side and speaks.)

Gilbert: Sheriff Connors! You're the last person I expected to see here. What I mean is, . . .

Connors: I think I know what you mean, Reverend Gilbert. I heard the music playing and thought I'd give a listen.

Gilbert: *(Looking toward area where music is coming from.)* Yes, I'm a music lover myself. But now tell me, *(Leading Connors to another area on stage.)* is there some other reason why you just happened to "wander" into the church?

Connors: Actually, there *was* something I wanted to speak with you about.

(Music fades out.)

I suppose you've heard about Mr. Slade's robbery.

Gilbert: Yes, I heard about it last night, a while after I got back.

Connors: Oh, have you been out of town?

Gilbert: *(Good-humoredly.)* Sheriff, if you were to spend a bit more time around this building, you'd be aware of what's going on in the church. Our congregation decided to sponsor a series of afternoon tent meetings down in Silverton. I just finished the last one yesterday.

Connors: Hmm. Seems like you would've stayed over in Silverton last night, bein' that you sermonized that afternoon and all.

Gilbert: I would've liked to, as I *was* plum tuckered out from all the singing and preaching. But I had the prayer-meeting service here in Eureka last night. So I rode on back, tired as I was. I reckon that's just part of doing the Lord's work.

Connors: I suppose so. Well, I'd better be moving along, Reverend.

Gilbert: I'm always glad when you're able to stop by, Sheriff, even if it is for just a few minutes.

Connors: *(Nods cordially.)* So long, Reverend.

Gilbert: Oh, and good luck in trying to catch the culprit who robbed Mr. Slade.

(Connors nods again and begins walking away. The Reverend Gilbert closes the door, and sings a couple bars of "Bringing in the Sheaves" as he exits. Upon hearing the tune, Connors stops dead in his tracks. He then glances back toward the church. After a brief moment of pondering, he turns and resumes his narration while walking.)

Connors: As Reverend Gilbert's voice faded away, I was reminded that I had yet to begin my search for the outlaw involved. But right now, my investigation was focused on Mr. Slade's mysterious benefactor. I stored the important points of this encounter in the back of my mind, and walked on to the Pittman residence. *(Pittman begins studying a set of plans he has been holding.)* Mr. Pittman, after greeting me, began to unfold his plans for an expanded railway system on the western side of the Rockies.

(Connors drifts over to Pittman, who begins speaking.)

Pittman: *(Rolling plans back up.)* Personally, I can't think of a reason why anybody would object to the plan, Sheriff. Oh, I suppose there's the usual person who thinks I don't offer a fair price for the land. But I do my best when it comes to making a bid.

Connors: I'm sure if anybody has a strong enough feeling about your idea they'll let you know.

Pittman: The real problem is that certain people have been asking John Slade to appraise their land. For some "strange" reason, Slade's appraisals are running unusually high. I won't speculate as to how generous Slade's clients might be with him should they get the price *he* sets on their land.

Connors: Suggesting that Mr. Slade is taking money under the table is a pretty strong accusation. Do you have any evidence to back it up?

(During Pittman's reply, Connors gives the muddy coat a suspicious glance.)

Pittman: I'll have to admit I don't, Sheriff. But just to make sure I don't run into any problems like that, I've decided to have a look at all the properties myself. That way I'll know for sure how much a particular piece of land is worth. As a matter of fact, I've been out of town all week doing that very thing.

Connors: Oh? When did you get back into Eureka, Mr. Pittman?

Pittman: Just last night. I spent the afternoon having a look at some land just outside of Silverton. I hear John Slade has already seen the same piece of property. It will be interesting to see how our appraisals compare.

Connors: I'm curious about something. When you travel, do you take a buggy or go on horseback?

Pittman: The places I usually go are too rugged for a buggy. Unless I have business strictly in town, I always take a good, strong horse.

Connors: Your Palomino?

Pittman: Not anymore. I sold that horse about a week ago. Picked up a good quarter-horse though. I have to admit I wouldn't have minded being in a buggy last night, though. I left Silverton late, about ten o'clock as I recall, and wouldn't you know it? It started raining just outside of town and stayed with us all the way to Eureka.

Connors: Well, maybe by this time next year that trip will be a little easier, assuming there's a train running between Silverton and Eureka.

Pittman: *(Determined.)* And there will be, unless John Slade proves to be more difficult to deal with than I expect he will.

(Mysterious piano interlude. Pittman exits, Connors walks away and continues his narration.)

Connors: At first, I thought the Palamino tip was a bum steer. But Mr. Pittman had told me enough to cause me to feel I was nearing the end of my investigation. Putting the pieces together had given me a clearer picture as to the identity of the person I had been tracking. There was, however, one more person I needed to speak with. Frank Littleton, the piano player over at the Grant Hotel restaurant.

(At this point, Connors makes his way over to the person who has been playing the piano during the scenes and begins speaking to him/her.)

In other words, you were the one who discovered Mr. Slade lying in the lobby last night.

Littleton: That's right, Sheriff. It was my night off, actually. But yesterday Miss Perkins asked me if I could fill in late for her on the desk.

Connors: And did you oblige?

Littleton: I told her I'd be glad to. I finished up entertaining the afternoon crowd and then headed out to play some checkers with Billy Johnson. After he'd beat me a couple of games I came back into town and caught a few winks of sleep. I woke up just before it was time to go work the desk, so I hurried on over to the hotel. Miss Perkins was just coming out the backdoor, so I went directly to the lobby. That's when I found Mr. Slade.

Connors: Let me ask you one other thing. You mentioned you went to play some checkers with Billy Johnson. Did you meet him at his place or somewhere else?

Littleton: We played over at his place, about a mile and a half out on the Silverton Trail.

Connors: Thanks. That's all I needed to know.

(Mysterious piano in background. Connors then continues the narration.)

It had been a difficult job, but I had heard and seen enough to be able to name the individual who had brought Mr. Slade back into town. The time had come to reveal my conclusions to the people I had questioned. (*All characters reenter, questioning each other as to the reason for their summons.*) Shortly, one of them would be exposed as the Samaritan of the Silverton Trail. But then, perhaps *you* already know who that is . . . ?

(*Music out. Connors clears his throat loudly to gain the group's attention. He then addresses them.*)

I hope you haven't all come here expecting your sheriff to name the individual who robbed Mr. Slade. I *could* do that, because that person was arrested a little while ago down in Silverton trying to pawn Mr. Slade's pocket watch. (*Group speaks approval to each other.*) But I have a more important reason for asking you to come here.

Every person in this room was on the Silverton Trail the evening of the robbery. You undoubtedly know that *someone* found Mr. Slade on the side of the road, bandaged his wound, and brought him into town. That person then left without being recognized for his or *her* actions. (*Connors glances at Lucille.*) It's been the purpose of my investigation to bring that person to light. Such an individual deserves to be caught. (*Group mumbles to each other in amazement.*)

(*Connors steps over to Miss Perkins and speaks to her.*)

It would not be surprising to find Miss Perkins doing such a thing. She's a fine and considerate lady.

Lucille: Thank you, Sheriff, but . . .

Connors: (*Interrupting.*) I think I know what you're going to say. There was a reason why Miss Perkins could not have done *this* good deed.

Lucille: Why, of course.

Connors: In talking with you, I realized that you had said you had returned to the Grant Hotel for supper. You then worked at the front desk for the rest of the evening.

Lucille: That's right, Sheriff.

Connors: The robbery, however, occurred last *night*, as Mr. Slade indicated. Since you were here in town during that time, you cannot be the person responsible.

(Piano chord, group agrees. Note: From here on, each successive piano chord should be slightly higher in pitch than the previous one. This helps build tension.)

Pittman: *(Points to Eustace.)* What about that old prospector there?

(Connors moves toward Eustace and speaks.)

Connors: I was particularly interested in Eustace's story, as he indicated that he was also on the Silverton Trail yesterday. But he told me that a Palomino horse and its rider had kicked up dust in his face. Obviously, the rain hadn't yet begun to fall. But Mr. Slade said it *was* raining at the time of his robbery. Because of that, I'm ruling out Eustace as the Samaritan of the Silverton Trail.

(Another piano chord, group again nods in agreement.)

Eustace: I know! *(Eustace points toward the Reverend Gilbert.)* The preacher! I think that's who you're alookin' fer, Sheriff. If'n anybody's got a serious concern for people, it's a preacherman.

Connors: Reverend Gilbert, as some of you know, has been down in Silverton holding tent meetings. He told me that he, too, was on the trail last evening. *(To Gilbert.)* After our visit earlier today, I heard you singing "Bringing in the Sheaves," a tune that Mr. Slade thought he heard as he lay beside the road. But Reverend Gilbert was already back in Eureka getting ready for the prayer meeting.

Gilbert: True enough, Sheriff. But "Bringing in the Sheaves" *was* the song I chose for the call at the end of my tent meeting yesterday. Whoever Mr. Slade heard singing was probably someone returning from the meeting.

(Piano chord, group again supports the verdict.)

Slade: Well, I know that cowhand Krebs wouldn't have stopped to help me!

(Connors now moves toward Joe Krebs and speaks.)

Connors: Joe Krebs was also on that same road last night.

Krebs: It's like I told you, sheriff. I was all riled up about what Daisy Mae had told me. I just had to get my brain aired out.

Connors: I remember. You said you rode out of town, heading south on the Silverton Trail. But you also told me that you rode in the moonlight. It would be pretty hard to see the moon if it were pouring down rain, as Mr. Slade said it was when he was robbed. No, it was somebody else who took it upon himself to bring Mr. Slade into town. It was either Mr. Pittman or Frank Littleton.

(Dramatic piano chord, Connors then moves over to Littleton and speaks.)

Frank Littleton told me that last evening, before he took a nap, he went to play checkers with Billy Johnson. As most of you know, Billy lives along the Silverton Trail.

Lucille: But, Sheriff, Billy Johnson lives just a mile and a half outside of town. Mr. Slade was robbed clear down at Adobe Bend. Why, that's a good seven and a half miles away!

Connors: You're exactly right, Miss Perkins. And that means that there's only one person here who could have done the act in question. *(Dramatically.)* Mr. Reginald Pittman.

(At this point, the piano hits a dramatic "sting" chord. The immediate characters on either side of Pittman then step aside in a bold move and look at him.)

Pittman: You'll never be able to prove that, Sheriff.

Connors: There is overwhelming evidence to indicate that it was indeed you who took the time to bandage Mr. Slade's wounds and bring him into town.

Pittman: *(Defensively.)* Such as?

Connors: First of all, you said that it was raining as you left Silverton last night, and that the rain stayed with you as you rode. That means it was raining at Adobe Bend when you were there. That wasn't true of anyone else.

Pittman: *(Nervously.)* But that still doesn't prove I brought Slade into town.

Connors: But something else does. *(Moves toward coat hanging on coat-rack.)*

(At this point, the piano begins playing a slow, successively higher single note. Again, this is to build tension.)

When I visited you earlier, I noticed your coat was wrinkled and muddy. That's because you were wearing that coat during your ride. The rain would have left the coat looking like that.

Pittman: *(More nervous.)* I *said* it was raining. That doesn't prove anything.

Connors: The wrinkles, no. But the mud on the coat's tail is a dead giveaway.

Pittman: I told you it was raining the whole way. I could've picked up that mud anywhere along the trail.

Connors: I'm afraid you're wrong. In the first place, you'd have to dismount for your coat to drag in the mud. But more importantly is the color of the mud. You see, *(lifting the coat's tail)* there's only one place in these parts where a person can find soil this color. Adobe Bend.

(Another dramatic piano "sting.")

Pittman: *(Hesitates, then "gives in.")* All right, all right. It's true. I *did* bring you into town, Slade. *(Slade stands here if he has been sitting down.)* But it's not because I like the way you go about your business. The fact is, that's why I kept it a secret. I didn't want people getting the idea that you and I had been down in Silverton working out some kind of a "land deal."

Slade: I don't know what to say, Pittman. You saved my life. But I'm still not sure why you bothered to stop and help me.

Pittman: It was something I heard Reverend Gilbert say a few weeks back in his sermon. Try as I might, it just wouldn't go away until I did something about it.

Slade: I attend the same church you do. What could you have heard that I didn't?

Pittman: It was just one sentence he read out of the Good Book. It said we ought to *(With emphasis.)* "Do unto others as you would have them do unto you."

Slade: *(After pausing reflectively.)* I guess I had you figured wrong, Pittman; I had you figured wrong.

(The characters "freeze," and soft piano music comes up. This music stays up during the final narration. Connors finishes the drama by speaking to the audience.)

Connors: People talked for a long time after that about what Mr. Pittman had done for Mr. Slade. I was so intrigued by what I had learned during my investigation, I started attending the church services myself. Been at them pretty regular ever since. Of course, people kind of wonder from time to time what's happened to me. And if they come to me directly about it, I don't hesitate a bit to tell them the story of the Samaritan on the Silverton Trail.

(Connors exits, music ends.)

Thought Starters for "Samaritan on the Silverton Trail"

1. For what reason(s) do many individuals prefer not to become involved in another's misfortune?
2. Most people will never find a robbery victim lying beside the road. What are some other ways the Christian can become actively involved in ministering to others' needs?
3. Deep down inside, most of us want to be recognized for our acts of kindness. Is this an appropriate Christian response? Why or why not?
4. Are there ever times when ceasing to show an individual "brotherly love" is the best choice?
5. What changes might occur at your school or workplace should the admonition "Do unto others as you would have them do unto you" be taken seriously?

4

The Good News Investment Company

Characters

Investment counselor
Prospective client

Props

Desk
2 chairs
Bible
Pencil and paper

A wealthy young man, concerned for the future, once came to Jesus for advice. The encounter is recorded in Luke 18:18-25.

In "The Good News Investment Company," you'll learn what's *really* important when it comes to the proper use of your time and talents. Whether you have a little or a lot to give, the folks down at "Good News" offer a few suggestions on how to reap a bountiful return on your investment.

Suggested Scripture

Proverbs 11:28; Luke 18:18-30; I Timothy 6:9, 10

The setting is an office.

Client: *(Walks into office.)* Excuse me. Is this the Good News Investment Company?

Counselor: It certainly is. What can we do for you today?

Client: My friend, Alan Baldwin, told me you people down here know a lot about making sound investments. Now, level with me. Can you guarantee the ultimate return?

Counselor: Well, Mr. . . .

Client: Johnson.

Counselor: Mr. Johnson, we *do* have a fairly high rate of success.

Client: How high?

Counselor: For those who follow our advice closely, we've had a one hundred percent rate of return.

Client: Sure beats the nine percent I've been looking at. Let's talk.

Counselor: Gladly. Please have a seat. The best way for us here at Good News to help you is to first ask a few questions. Do you mind?

Client: For a one hundred percent rate of return I'll stand on my head if you'd like.

Counselor: That won't be necessary. Simply answering the following questions will get things moving in the right direction. *(Picks up a checksheet.)* Now, first of all, thinking back over the past few months, have you murdered anyone?

Client: *(Taken aback.)* Say what?

Counselor: Have you murdered anyone?

Client: What are you talking about? Of course I haven't murdered anyone! What kind of a question is *that*?

Counselor: *(Places a check on the checksheet.)* I can understand your surprise, but these are questions that will give us a better idea as to your investment history. Now, let me ask you this: Have you ever committed adultery?

Client: *(Stands in shock.)* I don't believe this! This has no bearing on my investments!

Counselor: Most prospective clients feel the same way you do when they go through the initial interview. I remember the look on your friend Alan's face when he first came to us. But as you undoubtedly know, he *did* supply all of the necessary information. So, back to the question of adultery.

Client: *(Sits back down.)* Well, I still don't understand, but, no, I haven't committed adultery.

Counselor: *(Checks it off.)* A negative in the adultery column. You're doing great. Now, the third question has to do with your shopping habits. The last time you were in a department store, did you steal anything?

Client: *(Irritated.)* These questions still seem terribly irrelevant, but no, I don't shoplift. I'm an upstanding citizen of this community.

Counselor: *(Again he checks it off.)* Does not steal. I can see that you've worked very hard in the past to insure your future. Now, tell me, do you have a tendency to obfuscate the truth?

Client: What are you talking about?

Counselor: Do you lie? Let's be honest about it.

Client: *(Highly irritated.)* I don't appreciate your implying that I'm a liar, but for the sake of expediency, no, I don't lie!

Counselor: *(To himself again, as he checks it off.)* Honesty gets the okay. Well, just a couple of more questions, and we'll be ready to recommend a specific course of action.

Client: You've already been pretty "specific" if you ask me.

Counselor: Yes, I suppose it appears that way. Now, have you ever been accused of cruelty to parents?

Client: Absolutely not! I've always treated my parents with great respect.

Counselor: An important virtue, indeed. Honors father and mother. *(Checks off item on list.)* Well, we've finally reached the last question in this section. Tell me, do you love your neighbor as yourself?

Client: It's funny you should bring that up. Just this morning I found my trash can had been tipped over again by the neighbor's dog. I started to get upset, but then I said to myself, "It's not really Bill's fault that his dog has a bad habit." So, yes, I believe I do love my neighbor as myself. *(The counselor checks this item off.)*

But I still don't understand what all this has to do with investments. Actually, everything you've asked me about I've *never* had any problems with, not even when I was a kid.

Counselor: You have been extremely cooperative thus far, and it's appreciated. Now we need just a little information regarding your personal assets. *(Uses another piece of paper to make notes as he goes along.)*

Client: Hey, now you're talking my language! It's been a hard climb to the top, but persistence has finally paid off. That's why I'm here.

Counselor: Could you give me a brief listing of your personal assets?

Client: With pleasure. My pride and joy is parked right outside. When was the last time you had a ride in a forty-thousand-dollar automobile?

Counselor: *(Looks out window.)* It's a beauty, all right. What about household items?

Client: I'm pretty well set there, too. As a matter of fact, I'm having a few friends over tonight to check out my new VCR. The satellite dish should be here next week.

Counselor: I get the picture. Last of all, I'd like to know about any real-estate holdings you may have.

Client: That's easy enough. First of all, there's my regular house. But a couple of years ago, I was under a great deal of stress at work. That's when I decided a summer home on Hideaway Bay would be a smart move. It sure is great to get away every once in a while.

Counselor: I think that's about all we need. Based on this information I believe we can give you some sound investment advice.

Client: Good. I came prepared. Would you like a check up front, or would you prefer to bill me?

Counselor: You're already taken care of in that respect. The price was paid quite some time ago.

Client: You mean, Alan paid for all this?

Counselor: No, not Alan. Another Friend.

Client: But I don't think I know anyone who would do that for me.

Counselor: Perhaps not yet.

Client: I'm getting a little bit confused. How about some straight investment advice?

Counselor: Very well. By combining the information gleaned from the questionnaire with the items listed on the asset sheet, I can indeed suggest something specific.

Client: What's that?

Counselor: It has to do with your Porsche.

Client: I think I get it. I should hang on to it until the value goes up, right?

Counselor: No, rather, you'll need to sell it.

(At this point, the counselor freezes his action. The client then stands up and speaks directly to the audience.)

Client: Sell my Porsche? Do you realize how many years of hard work it took for me to be able to have that car parked in my garage? There are probably some things in this world I could do without. But my car isn't one of them. Sell it? No way!

The client turns back around and faces the counselor, who in turn unfreezes.)

Listen, friend, I know you're supposed to have a good reputation for investment counseling, but I don't think *that* suggestion is for me.

Counselor: Such a move no doubt *appears* to be a bit drastic. But by selling the car, you not only receive an immediate monetary return, but more importantly, you're establishing a solid base for even greater returns in the future. And *that's* what's really important.

Client: Well, it doesn't make sense to me. What else have you got?

Counselor: *(Disappointed.)* The next piece of information pertains to the household items you listed. It concerns the VCR you recently purchased.

Client: *(Interrupting.)* Ingenious! I don't know why I didn't think of it myself. You're going to suggest I rent out my VCR on the nights I'm not using it, and invest the receipts, right? It's a small thing, but it's the little day-by-day investments that really pay off!

Counselor: You're right about that, but wrong about renting out the VCR.

Client: What, you think I should charge admission instead?

Counselor: No. You're going to need to *sell* the VCR.

(The counselor freezes his action as before, the client then rises again and speaks directly to the audience.)

Client: Right. I'm sure I'm going to part with the only source of relaxation I get during the week. Is it so bad to want to have a little get-together with some friends once in a while? I don't know where this whiz kid is coming up with these crazy ideas, but I *do* know one thing. I'm not about to let his so-called "advice" come between me and my friends.

(The client turns back around to the counselor, and the previous action resumes.)

Tell me something. Just how do you go about coming up with these great "insights"? Why, if you were over on Wall Street, you'd have been laughed off the block already.

Counselor: I realize that from some people's point of view these suggestions appear to be foolish. But let me share something with you. Many years ago the President of Good News Investment Company made an exceptionally bold move. Certain individuals questioned *his* judgment, too. But those who followed his career to the end came to realize that he'd made the investment of a lifetime. It's all right here in the stockholder's report. *(Holds Bible up.)*

Client: Sounds like he must've been into futures trading.

Counselor: In a sense you're right. At any rate, as a result of his experience, we're able to guarantee that you'll be one hundred percent satisfied with *your* investment. That is, if you choose to follow his plan.

Client: Your story is very quaint. But it goes against everything I've learned about investing. The idea is to get rich, remember, *not* end up in the poor house.

Counselor: Riches come in many forms.

Client: Yeah, and thanks to the form known as cold, hard cash, I've got a brand-new VCR—and I intend to keep it. *(Stands to leave.)* I think I've heard enough "good news" for one day. So unless you have any other advice. . . .

Counselor: There *is* one last thing to consider if you expect your investment to pay the highest dividends.

Client: *(Sarcastically.)* Perhaps my faith in Alan Baldwin's judgment can yet be salvaged. Pray tell, what is this last financial maneuver?

Counselor: You must learn to give to the poor.

Client: *(Stands to leave again.)* Sorry, Alan ol' boy, but three strikes is all anybody gets with me. *(Speaks more thoughtfully now to the counselor.)* Listen, I can appreciate the fact that your president once made a right move. But times change, you know.

Counselor: Times may change, but the principles I've been sharing with you don't. They're time*less*.

Client: That's your opinion. But I need a plan I can really bank on in case the going gets rough.

Counselor: Our plan is the best one around. It's as solid as the Rock it was built on.

Client: *(Leaving for good.)* Well, thanks for the advice. But I don't think I can make myself believe that a hundred percent guarantee and all of your other promises are for real. I kind of wish I could. But I've got too much to lose to take that kind of a risk. I guess I'll just keep on listening to E. F. Hutton and hope for the best. So long.

(The client exits, and the counselor speaks the next couple of lines to himself.)

Counselor: It seems to me that a hundred percent guaranteed return on your investment is pretty good news. It kind of makes you wonder why so many people choose to walk away from an offer like that, *(Turns and speaks directly to audience.)* doesn't it?

Thought Starters for
"The Good News Investment Company"

1. What did the rich young ruler in Luke 18:22 still "lack"?
2. True or false: A person should purposely avoid accumulating worldly possessions.
3. Why does Jesus say it is so difficult for a wealthy individual to enter the kingdom of God?
4. What are some "riches" worth striving for?
5. You have just inherited five hundred thousand dollars from a wealthy uncle. On a piece of paper, describe how you will invest the money.

5

Under Construction in the Congo

Characters

Clint Steed, explorer

Quanto, native equipment manager and translator

Bukura, chief of the Soso tribe

2 native villagers

Props

Appropriate safari attire for Steed

White shirt, shorts for Quanto

Backpack

Canteen

Binoculars

Machete

Blankets for wrapping around villagers

Notebook

Pen

Bible

Virtually all home builders agree that the most important part of a house is the foundation. Jesus, himself a master craftsman, used that analogy in the parable sometimes known as "The Wise and Foolish Builders," found in Matthew 7:24-27. Here he points out the need to build your life's foundation based on heaven's stable principles.

"Under Construction in the Congo" finds explorer Clint Steed sharing that truth with a unique audience. By the time your viewers return from their journey through the jungle, they'll undoubtedly agree that it makes a great deal of sense to build on solid rock!

Deuteronomy 32:3, 4; Psalm 61:2; Matthew 7:24-27;
1 Corinthians 3:10–15

The skit opens with Steed entering, followed immediately by his helper, Quanto. Steed is carrying the canteen.

Steed: It was wise to suggest a drink of refreshing water, Quanto. The stifling heat of the Congo shows mercy to no one, not even I, Clint Steed, jungle explorer.

(The two halt, and Steed hands the canteen to Quanto. The former looks off into the distance.)

Quanto: Heat remind me of fiery furnace you speak of when telling story of Daniel found in Bible.

Steed: Indeed it does, Quanto. And speaking of fire, *(Points.)* look over there in the distance. The smoke rising from the valley suggests human activity. It's likely that it's a village, but the chance exists that the smoke indicates distress. We shall make that area our next destination.

Quanto: We go now.

(As the two proceed toward the area, the natives enter and assemble to await their arrival.)

Steed: *(Nearing natives.)* What we have here is another example of how drastically perception of distance can be affected near the equatorial zone. I was quite certain that we had at least a four-hour journey ahead of us. But I see we have arrived much sooner than I estimated.

Quanto: See that. But me not recognize markings on villagers' faces. Think best we do as Lot's wife in Bible and turn back. If not, could be in deep tribal trouble soon.

(Bukura, the village chief steps forward and lifts his hand to demand attention.)

Bukura: *(Points to himself.)* Me Bukura, capo Sosos.

Steed: Are you able to translate, Quanto?

Quanto: *(Translating to Steed.)* Yes, bwana. Say name Bukura. He chief of Soso tribe.

Steed: *(Excited.)* Quanto! We have stumbled across something of tremendous significance here.

Quanto: What that be?

Steed: Subscribing to a tribal philosophy of compromise, the Sosos were believed by most to have died out long ago. Recently, however, I read a theory suggesting that a few Sosos might remain. Unless I am mistaken, it appears that such conjecture may be more fact than fiction. Quanto, the survival of this people may well depend on our ability to show them the importance of rebuilding their societal structure from the ground up. But first things first. Ask the chief about the origin of the smoke we saw from the crest of the hill. Was it a village oven or has there been an accident?

Quanto: Bukura, toko loco smoko. It be bake bake or boo boo?

Bukura: Nasa. Bush go bye-bye. Saw saw, tack tack. Bukura gata hut.

Quanto: Bukura say neither oven nor mishap. Tribesmen clearing land to erect new hut for Bukura. Smoke come from burning bush. Remind me of story of Moses in Bible.

Steed: I am glad you remember the narrative, Quanto, but now ask the chief where the site of the proposed construction may be found. Unless I am mistaken, this is just the opportunity we seek to help save the Sosos from demise.

Quanto: Bukura, hoto goto saw saw tack tack?

Bukura: *(Motioning.)* Come quat.

Quanto: *(To Steed.)* We go now.

(The entire group follows Bukura to another point on stage. Bukura raises his hand to stop the procession.)

Bukura: *(Points downward.)* Dig dig.

Quanto: Chief Bukura say foundation go here.

(Steed bends low and scoops up an imaginary soil sample.)

Steed: *(Briefly surveys the sample.)* It's as I suspected, Quanto. The chief's selection of a construction site is a typical Soso choice. The soil is much too sandy here and will result in an unstable foundation. We shall ask the chief why an ill-advised location such as this was chosen over one of more stability, *(Looks around, then points.)* such as that nearby plateau area.

Quanto: Bukura, bwana Steed ta dig dig yuk yuk. *(Points to plateau area.)* What mata flata?

Bukura: *(Gestures toward adjacent area, then chuckles.)* Bwana Steed maka he he. Flata toofa to go. Hop to top, ta ho-hum come. *(Shakes head, then points decidedly to present area.)* Sosos dig dig. Nomo. *(Crosses arms to signify finality of decision.)*

Quanto: *(To Steed.)* Chief amused at bwana Steed's ignorance. Bukura say plateau too far from village. Workers tired by time reach site. Say put foundation here.

Steed: Intuition suggests that exhaustion is not the underlying issue. The chief's response is merely a reflection of the Soso tradition of unmitigated compromise. True, building the foundation on solid ground *(Nods toward plateau.)* would require more effort. But laying groundwork in soil such as this will result in the structure collapsing with the arrival of the monsoon season. It would be a foolish builder indeed who chose to build a house on shifting sand. The wiser choice would be an area such as the plateau, *(Points toward plateau area.)* where a person could build on solid rock.

Quanto: What bwana say make sense, but me not know best way to make Chief understand.

Steed: *(Reflects briefly, then speaks.)* I have an idea, Quanto. Cross-cultural communication of a concept such as this is sometimes possible through rhymed verse. Perhaps this would be an appropriate time to employ such a method. It is most critical that this tribe realize that the tradition of their past can only jeopardize their future.

Quanto: Quanto try bwana Steed's idea. *(To chief.)* Bukura,

(Here Quanto uses gestures similar to that which would be used in a children's song—first pointing to the ground, then his head, and so forth.)

Build hut on sand
It not be smart,
Hut fall to ground
When big rain start.

(Now points to plateau area.)

But build on rock
And you be wise,
Your hut stand firm
When waters rise!

(Bukura strokes chin and reflects momentarily. He then speaks, with the ensuing rhyming lines spoken in rapid succession.)

Bukura: *(Nodding head.)* Me now see.

Natives: *(In unison.)* So do we.

Quanto: *(To Steed.)* Three agree. Chief and villagers decide to build on solid ground.

Steed: Your poetic picture has prompted the Sosos to make a most intelligent decision. Please tell them this.

Quanto: *(To group.)* Bwana Steed taka Bukura tribe wise guys. *(They nod.)*

Steed: Quanto, we have shown the Sosos a better way of life. Hopefully, they will continue to build on solid ground, but the decision must be left with them. As for you and me, we shall move on. Please bid the chief farewell.

Quanto: *(Raises hand, Bukura reciprocates.)* Bukura, chief of Sosos, bwana Steed and Quanto gogo. *(Both lower hands.)*

(The Sosos wave good-bye and exit, Quanto and Steed turn in the opposite direction. Steed halts almost immediately.)

Steed: Quanto, I suddenly feel that this incident should be recorded for the benefit of future generations. Perhaps the written story of this encounter is destined to be left behind as my legacy to humanity. Lest I forget any significant details, I shall immediately jot a few notes in my journal. Please retrieve it for me.

(Quanto pulls the journal out of the backpack. The pen is attached.)

Quanto: *(Hands journal to Steed.)* Here book. But Quanto need say something.

Steed: *(Beginning to write in journal.)* Yes, Quanto, what is it?

Quanto: *(In cadence.)*

> What bwana Steed think
> Make a good story,
> Bound not to bring him
> Much fame and glory.

(Steed looks quizzically over at Quanto, pen still in hand.)

> For Quanto must tell you
> Though you may shed tear,

(Quanto quickly pulls the Bible out from the backpack, a pained expression crossing his face.)

> This story been told
> By Jesus, *(Points to Bible.)* in here!

Steed: *(Embarrassed.)* Uh, yes, I believe you're quite correct. *(Closes journal.)* Such being the case, a phrase undoubtedly spoken by Moses on the eve of the exodus seems appropriate.

Quanto: What that be?

Steed: *(Looks directly at Quanto.)* "We go now."

(Steed exits, followed immediately by Quanto.)

**Thought Starters for
"Under Construction in the Congo"**

1. Why is a sound foundation important?
2. How does a person lay a solid Christian "foundation"?
3. What are some possible reasons why certain individuals end up building their lives on "sandy soil"?
4. Is there such a thing as a "shortcut" to Christian character?
5. What is the best way to help someone you sense is developing questionable character traits?

6

Welcome Home

John 14:1-3 leaves the reader with an unmistakable message: Jesus is coming back. That's good news for some individuals, but bad news for others. It all depends on whether or not you're ready for his return.

In a most "surprising" way, "Welcome Home" shows the importance of being prepared for such a once-in-a-lifetime event.

Characters

Ted Maxwell

Theresa Maxwell

Leon Boerwinkle

Mr. Maxwell

Mrs. Maxwell

Props

Easy chair

A television

Several pop cans or bottles

A few comic books and magazines

A plate with spaghetti, a couple of lettuce leaves, a slice of bread, and a fork on it

Large bag of potato chips

Shirt and pants

Schoolbooks

Throw rug

Magazine rack

3 doughnuts (one regular, one
    doughnut hole, one jelly)

Luggage

Hawaiian shirt

Suggested Scripture

Matthew 25:1-13; Mark 13:32-37; John 14:1-3;
  2 Peter 3:8-10

The stage is set up as a living room, which is in complete disarray. The skit opens with Ted, dressed in gym clothes, plopped comfortably in the easy chair. He is watching TV and drinking a can of pop. Theresa enters carrying her schoolbooks.

Theresa: *(Surprised.)* Ted! What are you doing home already? I thought you had P.E. class at this time.

Ted: I do. But Mr. Smith sent us out for a run, so I decided to run home and watch "He-man."

Theresa: *(Disgusted.)* I don't believe you! Do you actually think you can get away with something like this?

Ted: *(Shifts attention toward Theresa.)* Oh, sure. There are so many guys in the class I'll never be missed. *(Stands and flexes muscles.)* Besides, do you really think *I* need to waste my time in a physical education class?

Theresa: Well, now that you mention it, your body *does* resemble a certain cartoon character that you're very fond of.

Ted: *(Surprised.)* Oh? Do you really think I look like He-man?

Theresa: I was referring to Bugs Bunny. *(Ted shrugs off the remark.)* Look, Ted, I just don't understand how you can sit there and watch TV when you know Mom and Dad are coming home tomorrow. If you're going to skip class, you could at least use the time to clean your mess up. *(Gestures around room.)*

Ted: Relax. I've got plenty of time. How long can it take to get the house in order?

Theresa: I suppose you're right. Maybe I'm being too hard on my little brother. I really should be complimenting you on how neatly you've kept the living room. After all, this disaster area looks immaculate compared to your bedroom.

Ted: *(Raises a suspicious eyebrow.)* How do *you* know what my room looks like? *(Grows irritated.)* You know good and well my room is "off limits" to all female siblings, of which you are the only one!

Theresa: I didn't need to go *into* it. Your room has just been kind of "creeping" out your door and down the hallway toward mine.

Ted: Aw, c'mon, ease up a little, would ya? By the time Mom and Dad get back from their trip, I'll be ready.

(Theresa shakes her head as she walks into the kitchen. There is a knock on the door.)

Ted: *(Opens door.)* Leon! *(The two slap hands. Leon has Ted's clothes with him.)*

Leon: Hey, Ted. *(Looks toward TV.)* How's He-man doing?

Ted: *(Irritated.)* I don't know anymore, thanks to my meddlesome sister. *(Turns TV off.)* So, did you have any trouble getting my clothes out of the locker room?

Leon: Naw, it was a piece of cake. *(Hands clothes to Ted.)* Speaking of that, do you have any more of those doughnuts we had last night?

Ted: I think there are a couple more around here someplace.

(Here Ted walks briefly around the room trying to locate the missing doughnut. Finally, he steps on the throw rug that hides it. He immediately halts. Note: The doughnut can be flattened prior to the performance. It is kept sanitary by placing it in a plastic sandwich bag. Simply lift the rug during the skit to hide the removal of the doughnut from the bag.)

Oh, yeah, I remember where they are now.

(He reaches down and picks up a flattened doughnut. He then hands it to Leon.) Here you go.

Leon: Thanks. *(Takes bite, then strolls over and looks out window.)* By the way, when did you say your parents would be coming home from their trip?

Ted: Sometime tomorrow. I hate to admit it, but I'm kinda looking forward to the folks getting back—especially Mom. I'm ready to fire Chef Boyardee.

Leon: *(Still gazing nonchalantly out window.)* Well, I've been doing some thinking. You know how we've been talking about picking up a used van and heading out west this summer?

Ted: Yeah?

Leon: Well, I suddenly feel that we should move our trip up.

Ted: Oh, really? Like to when?

Leon: Like to right now.

Ted: Are you crazy? I don't have enough cash to pay my library fines, let alone buy a van! Besides, I'm not even sure my parents will let me go.

Leon: Well, I suppose you could always ask them, since they just pulled in the driveway.

Ted: What are you talking about?

Leon: I'm talking about those two grown-ups who hang around here and occasionally refer to you as their son. They're sitting out in the car.

Ted: *(Becomes excited.)* What? Mom and Dad are back? That's impossible! They're not supposed to get in until tomorrow!

Leon: Unless each of your parents has an identical twin, it appears tomorrow is here a day early.

(Ted rushes over to the window and looks out.)

Ted: I can't believe it! It *is* them!

Leon: Yeah, but they're just sitting out there. I wonder what they're doing.

Ted: *(Panicky.)* I'll tell you what they're doing. They're listening to Paul Harvey. He always comes on the radio at this time of the day. *(Distraught.)* As soon as he's finished, they'll be ready to come in. Do you realize what this means?

Leon: Boy, do I. It means your father will want us to help him unpack the car. I think I'd better be moving . . .

Ted: No, you potato head! It means if I don't get this place cleaned up in the next three minutes we can forget about any trip this summer. In fact, *I* can forget about going *any* place for the next twenty years. I'll be grounded until I'm thirty-five!

Leon: Precisely the reason I was suggesting we head west, young man.

Ted: No, that'll never work. The important thing here is to stay calm. Look, I'm going to do what I can to stash all this trash. You stall my parents at the door until I give you the okay. Okay?

Leon: *(Hesitant.)* But what'll I talk about?

Ted: *(Quickly begins to hide pop cans in the magazine rack.)* You'll think of something. Just don't let them into the house until I give you the signal.

Leon: Well, it looks like I won't have much of a chance to rehearse my lines. They're already getting out of the car.

Ted: You know what to do!

(Ted rushes around trying to clean up the living-room area. He shoves the unopened bag of potato chips under the seat cushion of the easy chair. The plate of spaghetti is hidden under the chair. Leon moves over to the door where the Maxwells are about to enter. There is a jangling of keys, and the two parents appear with their luggage.)

Leon: *(Feigning surprise.)* Mr. and Mrs. Maxwell! You must be back from your trip.

Mr. Maxwell: *(Wearing Hawaiian shirt.)* Well, yes, Leon, as a matter of fact we are.

Mrs. Maxwell: So, how are you, Leon? We certainly missed you while we were gone.

(Mr. Maxwell tries to enter, Leon quickly glances back at Ted's progress, then prevents Mr. Maxwell from entering.)

Leon: Oh, I'm just fine. Say, Mr. M., that's a fine looking shirt you're wearing. Is it a souvenir from your trip?

Mr. Maxwell: No, I don't believe this look is native to Cleveland. But we did bring you each a little something from Ohio. *(Attempts to enter.)* Let me just set these bags inside and . . .

(Leon again blocks the way.)

Leon: Ohio, huh? Isn't that where they have the big surfing championship every year?

Mrs. Maxwell: I believe you're thinking of Oahu, Leon.

Leon: That's possible. Ohio must be where they hold that famous horse race.

Mrs. Maxwell: You mean the Kentucky Derby?

Leon: That's the one.

Mrs. Maxwell: No, I believe that's held somewhere in the South.

Mr. Maxwell: Tell you what, Leon. We have a complete set of World Book encyclopedias *(With emphasis.) inside.* I'd be glad to get you the one on horse racing just as soon as we . . .

(Ted has finished "straightening" the front room. He now comes over to greet his parents.)

Ted: *(Interrupting)* Mom! Dad! Welcome home!

Mr. Maxwell: Thank you, son. Would you mind giving us a hand with our luggage?

Ted: Of course not.

(Ted motions to Leon that it's all right to allow his parents to enter now. He then takes his mother's cosmetic case, much to Mr. Maxwell's chagrin.)

(While entering.) So, how did Aunt Millie's operation go? I mean, did everything come out the way it was supposed to?

Mr. Maxwell: In a manner of speaking, yes.

Ted: I guess it must've gone pretty well, since you came home a day early.

Mrs. Maxwell: *(Looking around.)* Well, to be honest with you, your father and I weren't sure how well you and Theresa would be able to handle both going to school and keeping the house in shape. But from the looks of things, we needn't have worried.

Mr. Maxwell: Yes, I must admit the place looks to be in tip-top shape. It's particularly encouraging since you thought we wouldn't even be coming back until tomorrow.

Leon: Yep, that's Ted. Always prepared for the unexpected.

(Ted gives Leon a disapproving glance.)

Mrs. Maxwell: Say! We haven't even said hello to Theresa yet. Where is she?

(Theresa enters from kitchen.)

Theresa: I'm right here!

Mrs. Maxwell: Well, I was beginning to wonder if these two men had banned you from the house! I'm glad to see you, Honey. We missed you.

Theresa: I missed you both, too. But it was Ted who really felt the separation.

Mrs. Maxwell: Oh, really? What makes you say that?

Theresa: Well, I've been watching from the kitchen for the last few minutes, and unless I'm mistaken, Ted has planned a little "welcome home" celebration for you. Isn't that right, Ted?

Ted: Huh?

Theresa: Oh, don't be so bashful about it. You've gone to a lot of trouble getting ready for Mom and Dad's return. Now, go ahead and let them in on your secret.

Ted: What are you talking about?

Theresa: Well, if you're not going to get the party rolling, I will! *(Theresa heads toward the chair.)* First, for Dad, a dish prepared from one of Ted's favorite recipes—

(Theresa flamboyantly pulls out the plate of spaghetti from underneath the chair.)

Pasta a la Penicillin, with a Seizure Salad and a slice of garbage bread!

(She hands the plate to Mr. Maxwell who grows queasy.)

Ted: Theresa!

Theresa: Of course, there's more where that came from. Mom, if you'll just sit down in this chair, our host has prepared yet another delicacy in honor of your return.

(Mrs. Maxwell sits down hard in the chair. Upon feeling the bulk underneath her, she immediately lifts the cushion and pulls out the potato-chip bag.)

That's right, Smashed potatoes!

Leon: *(Apprehensively.)* Teddy, I think the proverbial chips are down.

Ted: *(Fuming.)* Theresa, I'd like to have a few words for you, I mean, *with* you out in the kitchen.

Theresa: I'll be there in a minute. But first, I'm sure you want Mom and Dad to enjoy their special dessert, don't you?

(Theresa bends down and lifts up a corner of the rug. She retrieves a doughnut hole and a jelly doughnut.)

Here's a hairy doughnut hole for mom, and a belly-up jelly doughnut for you, Dad. If either of you would like something to wash your treats down with, there's plenty of pop right here in the magazine rack. *(She reaches down and holds up a can of pop.)* I'll run out to the refrigerator and get you both a magazine to read while you enjoy your meal.

Leon: I think I'll be leaving now.

Ted: *(Through clenched teeth, he grabs Theresa by the arm.)* Good idea. And why don't you take "Theresa the Terrible" here along with you? *(Leon begins to leave, pulling Theresa along with him.)*

Mr. Maxwell: All right, everybody. Let's hold it right there!

(All of them suddenly pay attention to Mr. Maxwell.)

I'm beginning to get the picture. Theresa, what you've done to your brother is hardly praiseworthy.

Ted: Yeah . . .

Mr. Maxwell:	However, *(Ted is taken aback.)* I will have to say that I *am* disappointed in you, Ted.
Theresa:	Yeah . . .
Mr. Maxwell:	But I think both of you can benefit from what I'm about to say.
Leon:	Yeah! *(All look at Leon, he smiles sheepishly and shrugs his shoulders.)*
Mr. Maxwell:	I had, indeed, hoped that you would be ready for our return, Ted. But it's obvious your time has been spent in other areas.
Theresa:	His bedroom isn't one of them.
Mr. Maxwell:	*(Slightly scolding.)* Thank you, Theresa, but I'll handle this if you don't mind. *(To Ted again.)* I think the way you've kept house while we were away pretty much speaks for itself, son. It's unfortunate that you've chosen to let things get so out of hand in our absence. Nevertheless, I'm sure between you and your cohort in grime here *(Nods at Leon.)* you'll manage to have the situation rectified before you go to bed tonight. *(More forcefully.)* Am I not correct?
Ted:	I have no reason to doubt your word.
Mr. Maxwell:	But there's something more important than just a tidy house that I hope can be gained from the current state of affairs.
Ted:	What's that?
Mr. Maxwell:	Realizing the importance of being prepared for something that you know is eventually going to happen.
Leon:	Like somebody coming back, only sooner than expected?
Mr. Maxwell:	A perfect example, Leon.
Ted:	*(Shamefacedly.)* I guess I *was* kind of taking a risk. But couldn't you have at least called and told us that you were on your way home?
Mr. Maxwell:	I suppose I could have. But then, if you'd have been ready all along, it really wouldn't have mattered, would it?
Mrs. Maxwell:	*(After a slight pause.)* I think your father's point is this: The best way to be prepared for something is to spend a little time each

day getting ready for it. That way, you won't be taken by surprise. *(All nod in agreement.)*

Mr. Maxwell: Well, you gentlemen had better get started. You've got a big job ahead of you, to say the least. But, first, I'd appreciate a little help unpacking the car.

(Mr. Maxwell heads for the door, with Leon arriving there just before him.)

Leon: Uh, I'd like to help, Mr. Maxwell, but your talk has made a profound impression on me. It suddenly occurs to me that I have a history test tomorrow morning, and I still have twelve chapters to read. I realize now that if I'm going to ace that test, I'm going to have to be prepared. *(As he exits.)* So long, Mr. and Mrs. M. Oh, and welcome home!

(All step over to the doorway and watch Leon disappear down the street.)

Theresa: Can you believe a guy like that?

Ted: I'll say. I can't think of anybody else who would be stupid enough to put something that important off until the last minute.

(There is a slight pause as everyone turns his head and stares at Ted.)

(Embarrassed.) Well, heh-heh, *almost* nobody.

(Ted grabs the plate of spaghetti and quickly exits to the kitchen. The others simply shake their heads in disbelief.)

Thought Starters for "Welcome Home"

1. What are some biblical bases for believing that Jesus will soon return to this earth?
2. How should a person spend his or her time waiting for Jesus' return?
3. Jesus said in Matthew 24 that just before he came back life would be "as it was in the days of Noah" (*see* v. 37). Are there any indications that this might now be happening? If so, what are they?
4. For many individuals, the idea of Jesus' coming back to earth is hard to grasp. What are some reasons why this might be?
5. Why has Jesus waited this long to come back?

7

The Junkyard Jewel

Characters

Mike Holness, car restorer
Otto Graves, junkyard owner
Rusty Wheeler, automobile

Props

3 or 4 hubcaps
A couple of spare tires
Chair
Appropriate attire for characters

The gospels are filled with accounts of Jesus' healings. The stories of blind Bartimaeus, the ten lepers and the woman made well by touching the hem of Jesus' garment come immediately to mind.

Equally significant, though, are the numerous occasions where the spiritually sick were made whole. Nicodemus, Zaccheus, and countless others could testify of such miracles.

"The Junkyard Jewel" depicts such a transformation. By watching Rusty Wheeler go from junk to polished gem, your audience will pick up some valuable tips on the finer points of restoration.

Suggested Scripture

Psalm 23:3; John 3:1–21; 2 Corinthians 5:17

The skit opens with Otto polishing a hubcap in the junkyard office. The other hubcaps and spare tires are arranged as desired. Rusty is sitting in a chair on the opposite side of the stage. Mike enters.

Otto: Well, howdy, pardner. What can I do for you today? Got a special this week on Buick radiators.

Mike: Thanks, but I'm not in the market for one of those today. Actually, I'm looking for a car.

Otto: Well, cars is one thing I got plenty of. But if you need one that runs, you came to the wrong place.

Mike: I'm quite certain that I came to the right place. By the way, my name is Mike Holness, and I'm a restorer. *(Reaches over to shake hands.)*

Otto: Otto Graves here. Say, if you're a restorer, you might be interested in a '59 Cadillac I just got in. With a little tinkering and a new paint job, you'd have yourself a real classic.

Mike: That does sound interesting, but frankly, I'd like something a little more challenging.

Otto: Well, if it's a challenge you're looking for, I've got just the thing sittin' down at the far end of the yard. The upholstery is a little torn, and you'll have to find yourself a new bumper. But you don't find a '48 Hudson every day of the week.

Mike: I'm sure that would be ideal for many people. But I'd really like to find something that needs a total makeover. Maybe even something like *(Pauses, and points to Rusty.)* that one.

Otto: What? Have you slipped your gears? It's one thing to restore a car, but putting that hunk of junk back into shape would take a miracle!

Mike: I think I'm up to the task. If you don't mind, I'd like to take a closer look.

Otto: *(Resignedly.)* Be my guest. I'll be inside if you need anything.

(Otto shakes his head and walks away. Mike strolls over to Rusty.)

Mike: *(Talking to himself.)* It's been a while since I've seen one of these. The body is in pretty bad shape. It looks like there's still a little air left in this tire, though. *(Kicks Rusty's shin.)*

Rusty: Ouch! Take it easy. I may not look like much but that doesn't mean you can just kick me around.

Mike: (*Surprised.*) Well, another Talkswagen. This job should prove most rewarding.

Rusty: What job?

Mike: Perhaps I should introduce myself. My name is Mike Holness, and I'd like to restore you; that is with your consent, of course.

Rusty: Well, how do I know old Rusty Wheeler can trust you?

Mike: Believe me, Rusty, I know what I'm doing. Now, tell me honestly, wouldn't you like to be back on the road again?

Rusty: Sure I would. But I just don't have what it takes anymore.

Mike: No you don't, but I do.

Rusty: What are you going to do to me?

Mike: Well, the first thing we have to do is get you a new set of tires. That way, you'll be able to take the bumps a little better out there where the rubber meets the road.

Rusty: I do have to admit that I've had a pretty rough go of it on occasion.

Mike: Of course, that's just the beginning. With your permission, I'd like to do a ground-up restoration.

Rusty: What? I don't want to be ground up!

Mike: What I mean is, I want to do a complete overhaul. When it's time for you to be judged, a mere paint job won't carry much weight.

Rusty: Do you mean I'm going to be in a contest?

Mike: In a sense, yes.

Rusty: I'd like to think I could be a show car, but look at me. Why, before the wrecker brought me here, I was parked behind a barn for years. I've been sitting here in the rain and mud ever since. Are you sure I'm worth it?

Mike: Rusty, it doesn't matter where you've been or what you've been through. You may think you're just a piece of junk, but underneath your dents and scratches, I see a jewel.

Rusty: Well, one thing's for sure, I'm going no place fast sitting here. I guess it can't hurt to give you a chance. If you can really redeem me from this wrecking yard, I'll do my best to make a good showing for you.

Mike: It's a deal. But first we'll have to get you out of here and into the body shop. There they have specially trained people and plenty of tools to help in your restoration.

Rusty: But I thought you'd be doing the work yourself.

Mike: Rest assured that I'll be overseeing the project from start to finish.

Rusty: Well, you've convinced me. But I do have one more question.

Mike: What's that?

Rusty: When the job is completed, will you put me up for sale?

Mike: By that time, Rusty, I'll have far too much invested. No, I have other plans for your future.

Rusty: Not a dark, stuffy auto museum, I hope.

Mike: No. Rather a bright and airy destination. You see, I plan to take you home myself.

Thought Starters for "The Junkyard Jewel"

1. Is there a necessary first step one must take to be restored? If so, what is it?
2. What are some specific Bible incidents where people were spiritually restored?
3. In spiritual restoration, who does the work?
4. When is the process of restoration finished?
5. How can you tell whether or not you've been restored?

8

Sinner's Point

Characters

Wes, park visitor

Jungle Jim, tour guide

The Master, mask shop proprietor

Gate attendant

3 people to ride on "Jungle Jim's Guilt Trip"

Persons to ride on the "Emotional Roller Coaster"

Ride operator

Props

6 chairs

Microphone

Lone Ranger mask

Grocho Marx glasses/nose

Cassette tape player with recorded carnival music

Money

Some receipts

In numerous instances throughout his ministry here on earth, Jesus proved his willingness to both forgive *and* forget human mistakes. The story of the woman caught in the act of adultery, found in John 8:1-11, is but one example.

The Bible makes it clear that because of Jesus' death, forgiveness is now ours for the asking. But convincing ourselves of that fact is sometimes a difficult thing to do. Self-forgiveness, however, plays an important role in maintaining our emotional equilibrium.

"Sinner's Point" provides the perfect environment in which to learn more about this important topic. Within the confines of this unusual amusement park, your viewers will come to realize that not only is forgiveness something to be asked for, but it is something that we must accept.

Micah 7:19; John 8:1-11; Philippians 3:12-14;
1 John 1:9

The setting is an amusement park. The opening exchange occurs at the entrance gate. The carnival music is playing in the background.

Gate Attendant: Hello, and welcome to Sinner's Point Theme Park.

Wes: Thanks. I've never been here before.

Gate Attendant: Oh? Any particular reason you've waited this long?

Wes: Well, until just recently I never felt the need. But, you see *(Ashamed, leans in close.)* I've committed a . . . well, let's just say I've done something I'd give anything to *undo*.

Gate Attendant: Your situation is fairly typical.

Wes: Not that I haven't already done everything I could. But I just don't *feel* like it's enough. Fortunately, I happened to spot your color brochure at a rest area. It was a lot flashier than the one sitting right next to it. I'm convinced this is just what I need to make me feel better.

Gate Attendant: We do have a lot of rides that the other park doesn't. I'm sure you'll find something here to satisfy your particular needs.

Wes: Great! *(Reaches for wallet.)* I'll take an all-day pass to Sinner's Point.

Gate Attendant: *(Laughs.)* They use that kind of plan at the other park. But here at Sinner's Point you simply pay as you go.

Wes: *(Puts wallet back in pocket.)* Now that's my kind of plan. I'll just ask for a receipt at each turnstile, just in case I need to prove to anybody that I really paid up.

Gate Attendant: I thought you'd like it. Now, unless I'm mistaken, one ride you'll want to be sure and try is waiting for you right over there. *(Points.)* It's called "Jungle Jim's Guilt Trip."

Wes: That sounds like a good one for me. I think I'll go there first. Thanks for the tip.

Gate Attendant: Glad to be of assistance.

(The gate attendant leaves, and Wes heads over to "Jungle Jim's Guilt Trip." The "launch" consists of folding chairs arranged to accommodate four passengers. Jungle Jim serves as the turnstile agent. The boat is almost ready to leave. The carnival music fades out at this point.)

Jungle Jim: *(Shouting.)* Last call for "Jungle Jim's Guilt Trip."

Wes: *(Steps up pace.)* I hope I'm not too late. *(To Jungle Jim.)* Are there any seats left?

Jungle Jim: We always have room for one more.

Wes: Great! *(Hands Jim a bill.)* You can keep the change, but I do need a receipt.

Jungle Jim: Thank you. *(Hands him a receipt.)*

(Wes peruses the launch for the empty seat. Upon locating it, he sits down. Jungle Jim steps aboard.)
Welcome, fellow self-floggers, to "Jungle Jim's Guilt Trip." I'm Jungle Jim, and I'll be serving as your guide during our brief excursion into Upper Guiltia. So without further ado, let's fire up the launch and shove off, shall we?
(A good effect is to have one of the passengers or a person on the front row imitate the starting of the engine and its ensuing drone. Also, some tropical bird and animal sounds help to set the mood.)

Wes: *(To passenger in adjacent seat.)* Boy, this is pretty exciting. This is the first time I've ever been on this ride. How about you?

Passenger #1: *(Expressionless.)* I've been in this boat at least a hundred times before.

Wes: A hundred times! You must really enjoy it!

Passenger #1: Fact is, I hate it. But it's the best way I've found to help me enjoy my misery.

(Wes looks a little confused at his seatmate's remark.)

Jungle Jim: *(Speaking into microphone.)* Even as we begin our journey we see to our left *(All look to the left.)* a fine specimen of Upper Guiltia's rare tropical foliage, the Burden of Paradise.

All Passengers: Ohhh . . . !

Jungle Jim: And if you look closely, on the right *(All aboard turn to right.)* you'll discover wading close to shore an example of the area's unique wildlife, the Gray-bleaked Regret.

All Passengers: Ahhh . . . !

Jungle Jim: *(Grows serious.)* Ladies and gentlemen, we're now approaching the highlight of our tour. *(Points.)* The area to which I'm pointing was long ago an ancient ritual grounds for the Guiltian people. It was on this spot that, as an act of homage to the god of guilt, tribal members would beat themselves on their consciences. Interestingly, legend has it that this morbid tradition is carried on even today amongst the descendants of the Guiltians.

Wes: *(To seatmate.)* Come on. Does he really expect us to believe something like that?

Passenger #1: Jungle Jim's been at this a long time, ever since I started coming here. Take it from me, he knows what he's talking about.

Jungle Jim: And with that we wind our way back to dockside. *(Motor and sound effects end.)* I hope you've had an exciting and informative journey today on "Jungle Jim's Guilt Trip." See you next time!

(The passengers exit the boat.)

Wes: *(To former seatmate.)* You know, to be honest with you, that ride was a little disappointing. I don't feel a bit better. Say, since you come here all the time, what do *you* recommend?

Passenger #1: Well, I'm going on the Guilt Trip again. But everybody's different. Why don't you give the "Emotional Roller Coaster" a whirl? I've heard it's one of the most popular rides here.

Wes: Thanks. I think I'll go there right now.

(Wes heads over to the "Emotional Roller Coaster." The roller coaster car(s) consists of two chairs placed next to each other. The ride operator enters, along with another patron. The other rider(s) pays and gets in the car.)

Ride Operator: *(Loudly.)* Step right up for the ride of a lifetime. Grab a seat on the "Emotional Roller Coaster."

Wes: *(To operator.)* I'll have a ride. *(Hands him a bill.)*

Ride Operator: *(Gives him a receipt.)* Here you go. You can take that seat right there. *(Points to the empty seat.)*

(Wes sits down next to the previous customer.)

Wes: *(To seatmate.)* I don't know about you, but I'm a little nervous.

Passenger #2: Relax. Just hang with me, and I'll show you how it's done.

Wes: Oh, you've been on the "Emotional Roller Coaster" before?

Passenger #2: A few times. Of course, a person can only go on this ride so often. You'll see what I mean. By the time this ride is finished, you'll have been through more ups and downs than you ever thought possible.

(The ride operator comes over and pulls down an imaginary restraining bar.)

Ride Operator: If you're ready, so am I. Enjoy your ride.

(The operator starts the ride by flicking an imaginary switch.)

Passenger #2: Hang on, here we go!

(The two jolt in their seats as the ride begins.)

We don't go too far before the first real scare comes along. In fact, it's just ahead. *(Pauses.)* All right, *(Loudly, quickly.)* lean to the left!

(Both lean to the left, but Wes looks down to the right.)

Both: Whoaaa!

Passenger #2: Don't look down, you might faint! We're on the Ridge of Resentment.

Wes: *(Relieved, looking back.)* Whew! That seemed to come out of nowhere.

Passenger #2: It always happens that way. But that's nothing compared to what's ahead. When I give you the signal, shift your weight to the other side. *(Pauses.)* Okay, here comes the Edge of Anger! *(Shouts.)* Lean!

(Both lean to the right.)

Both: Whoaaa!

Wes: *(Fearful.)* I don't know. Maybe I shouldn't have . . .

Passenger #2: It's too late to turn back now. Hold on!

(Both lean back on the two rear legs of their chairs.)

We're headed up Anxiety Hill. This is bad enough, but what's on the other side is even worse.

Wes: *(Scared stiff.)* What's that?

(The two now level their chairs, and then lean forward to simulate a descent.)

Passenger #2: *(Shouting.)* The Deep Depression . . . *(Fades out as they "fall.")*

Wes: *(Shouting.)* I can't take anymore! Stop this thing! I've gotta get off!

(The ride operator steps forward and stops the ride. Wes steps out. The passenger shakes his head and walks offstage.)

(Breathing heavily.) What a terrible experience! Maybe other people like riding the "Emotional Roller Coaster," but it's sure not for me. I'm exhausted!

Ride Operator: It does require a certain amount of intestinal fortitude. *(Puts arm around Wes's shoulder.)* Listen, would you mind if I offered a suggestion?

Wes: I guess it can't hurt anything. I came here to help myself feel better, and nothing has worked yet. What do you have in mind?

Ride Operator: There's a certain shop over near Pain Street USA. It's called "Master in Disguise." I've never been there myself, but it sure sounds like the kind of place where a person could cover up his problem.

Wes: Say, that does sound like a possibility. I think I'll check it out.

(The ride operator exits offstage. Wes proceeds down the street, reading the signs along the way.)

Hmmm. *(Squinting.)* "Sinner's Point Original Twisted Knot Pretzels. Isn't it about time you put a Twisted Knot in your stomach?" That's not what I'm looking for. *(Spots another sign.)* Ah, this must be the place. "Master in Disguise—We Do Complete Makeovers."

(The Master enters from the opposite side of the stage. Wes enters the shop.)

The Master: Good afternoon, and welcome to "Master in Disguise."

Wes: Uh, yeah, thanks. I just hope you've got something here that can help me cope with my situation.

The Master: I'm certain that I can furnish you with a solution to whatever problem you may be facing. Just be sure and look things over carefully before making your final decision. I'll be glad to offer my assistance whenever you need it.

Wes: Sounds good to me. I never have liked the pushy approach. Now, let's see what my options are. *(Begins to peruse the merchandise.)* The important thing is to not give people the impression that I'm taking the easy way out. *(He spots the Lone Ranger mask.)* Hmmm. This looks like something I can hide behind and still feel like a man. *(Puts mask on.)*

The Master: A novel approach, indeed. But the truth is, a mask can never provide a permanent solution to your problem.

Wes: *(Removes the mask.)* You're probably right. It could eventually wear thin and somebody might see through it. I'd better go for something I can really rely on.

The Master: That's right.

Wes: And I think I've found it! *(Reaches for the Groucho Marx glasses, puts them on.)* Yes sir, one look at this and I'll have 'em rolling in the aisles! If this funny front doesn't do the trick, I don't know what will.

The Master: It would be a humorous approach. But what you're going through is hardly a laughing matter.

Wes: Since you put it that way, I guess my problem is a little more serious than that. *(Removes glasses, looks around.)* But, I don't see anything else to choose from. Is this all you have?

The Master: There is one other thing I can offer you.

Wes: What's that?

The Master: A way out.

Wes: But I just got here.

The Master: I'm not suggesting that you leave my presence. But, if you're like most people who come here, you're looking for a way out of the mess you've gotten yourself into. That's where I can help.

Wes: Well, you just happen to be right. *(With a ring of frustration and irritation.)* I've been up, down, and all around this stupid park trying to do my guilt in. I've tried riding it and hiding it, but nothing has worked. It seems like the "Suicide Bobsled" is about the only thing left.

The Master: I don't think that would be a very wise choice.

Wes: *(Sharply.)* Well, you sure haven't come up with anything better! *(Immediately grows apologetic.)* I'm sorry. I guess I've just had it up to here *(Gestures.)* with this guilty feeling. Please forgive me.

The Master: I already have.

Wes: What did you say?

The Master: I said, I forgave you the moment you first asked me to.

Wes: *(Pauses, then looks at the Master in amazement.)* Are you trying to tell me that you're *the* Master?

The Master: *(With a slight smile and nod.)* In disguise.

Wes: *(Taken aback, yet suspicious.)* Now, wait a minute. If you're really the Master, what in the world are you doing here at Sinner's Point?

The Master: I've found it's the perfect place to help certain individuals deal with the root of their problem. You see, bringing sinners to the point of being able to face themselves is what my business is all about.

Wes: But I still don't get it. If you've already forgiven me, why do I still feel so lousy?

The Master: It's really quite simple. You see, you haven't forgiven yourself.

Wes: *(Pauses reflectively, and draws a deep breath.)* I think this sinner is beginning to get the point.

The Master: *(Gently, placing arm around Wes's shoulder.)* In that case I believe you're ready to leave this Tragic Kingdom and start learning more about another one.

Wes: *(Walking together toward exit.)* Oh? What's it called?

The Master: Forgivenessland, a place where the only thing that stands between regretting and forgetting *(Pause for emphasis.)* is *you.*

(The action freezes, and the lights fade down and then out.)

Thought Starters for "Sinner's Point"

1. Does the Bible place any conditions on God's forgiveness? If so, what are they?
2. What are some things that might hinder an individual from being able to forgive him or herself?
3. Is guilt ever a good thing? If so, when?
4. If forgiveness is always available, why not take advantage of it and live a life of sinful pleasure?
5. The Bible speaks of one sin that is "unforgivable." (*See* Luke 12:10.) Just what kind of sin is it, and how is it committed?

9

Ticket to Heaven

Characters

Dewey Dewmore

Buddy Armbruster

Ticket agent

Props

Appropriate "rural" dress clothes for Buddy and Dewey

Suitcase

Notepad

Framed diploma

A choir robe

2 chairs (for car)

Steering wheel

2 airline tickets

Optional: Ticket counter

Some people will try almost anything to get to heaven—everything from flaunting their good deeds to getting their ticket punched based on someone else's performance.

But in John 14:6, Jesus makes it clear that there is only one way to gain citizenship in the heavenly kingdom—by choosing to accept what he has already done for us. Such is the lesson lifelong pals Dewey Dewmore and Buddy Armbruster learn in "Ticket to Heaven."

Suggested Scripture

Matthew 7:21; John 3:16, 17; 14:1-3, 6; Acts 4:10-12

The skit opens with Buddy and Dewey in a car, the former behind the wheel. Dewey carries his notepad with him.

Buddy: I got to admit, Dewey, when you get your head set on doin' somethin', a person would have more luck teachin' a mule to play the pianer than he would gettin' you to change your mind!

Dewey: I believe you might not be too far from right there, Buddy. I been plannin' this here trip for a mighty long time, and I ain't about to call it off now.

Buddy: Where was it you said you was goin' again?

Dewey: How in the world could ya forget somethin' like that? If I've told ya once I've told ya twice—I'm takin' a trip to heaven.

Buddy: I don't know how I could've forgot that! It sure ain't every day a feller's best friend plans to spend his vacation *there*!

Dewey: I 'spect you're right, Buddy. Previous to this, the closest I ever came to paradise was when I went to my cousin Ernie's wedding in Nashville.

Buddy: It's hard to believe it could get much better than that! By the way, are we gettin' close to where we turn off?

Dewey: The person I talked to on the telephone said we wasn't supposed to turn either left or right, that we should just keep on goin' straight. She said we'd know we was gettin' close, when we began to see the signs.

Buddy: Hey, looky there! That sign says Ruby Falls is just over yonder. What say we go take a quick look-see?

Dewey: What did I just tell ya? The lady said there's only one way to get there. If we just up and head off on our own, we're sure ta get ourselves lost. And besides that, we ain't got all the time in the world, ya know!

Buddy: I 'spose you're right. *(Looks at Dewey's suitcase.)* Now, you're sure you didn't forget anything?

Dewey: I'm pretty certain I've thought of everything. But I packed a few extras just in case somethin' important might of slipped my mind.

Buddy: *(Points ahead.)* Looks like that woman was sure enough right. There's the terminal straight ahead, but I don't know which door to take ya to.

Dewey: All she said was we'd know which one it was when we got there.

Buddy: *(Strains to read signs, then speaks excitedly.)* That must be it right there!

Dewey: *(Reading sign aloud.)* "Celestial City." I reckon that's the place we're lookin' for. Why don't ya pull over into the unloading zone?

(Buddy pulls over and parks. As both exit the car, Dewey picks up his suitcase.)

Well, no sense in standing here. Come on, let's go in.

(Dewey and Buddy go over and open the door. Once inside, they walk very closely next to each other. This is to portray the idea that they are walking down a narrow hallway. The suitcase is between them.)

Buddy: Between you, me, and the suitcase, there sure ain't much room in this hallway. Kinda gives me closetphobia.

Dewey: It does seem a mite narrow, doesn't it?

(The two reach the end of the hallway and once again walk a normal distance from each other.)

Buddy: *(Spots ticket counter and nudges Dewey.)* Dewey, there's the counter. I'll hang onto your suitcase while you go and get your ticket.

Dewey: *(Approaches ticket agent.)* Excuse me, ma'am, can I get a ticket to heaven here?

Agent: You've come to the right place. Have you made the necessary arrangements?

Dewey: *(Leans in close to agent.)* Well, actually, I'd like to speak to you about that. Down in Franklinsburg, where I come from, we have a little process called bartering. See, I don't have much money, but I got a few things I could trade for a ticket.

Agent: It's not our usual procedure, but we're anxious to give people every opportunity to make the trip. What exactly did you have in mind?

Dewey: When I first got the hankerin' to go on this trip, I decided I'd have to quit doin' the wrong things—like stoppin' off at the Whiskey Keg—and commence doin' the right kinds of things. I'd been reformed for almost a week, when I realized that I'd need more than my own word to prove that I was a changed man. So I ran right on over to the Dixie Five-and-Dime and bought myself a pad and pencil. I been keepin' a record ever since. Here, have a look. *(Hands notepad to agent.)*

Agent: *(Reading from notepad.)* "Tuesday night—drove right past the Whiskey Keg without battin' an eyeball. Later changed a flat tire for a Yankee tourist who was passin' through town."

Dewey: It sure ain't been easy livin' that kind of a life. But I figure if hard work is the price I have ta pay to get me where I'm goin', I'm willin' to put in my time.

Agent: Well, Mr. . . .

Dewey: Dewmore, Dewey Dewmore.

Agent: Mr. Dewmore, the changes you've made *are* for the better. Alcohol is a destructive drug, and giving it up will certainly make life easier for you and those around you. And helping others is a good way to show them you care. But, even though you've worked hard at living a better life, I'm afraid these changes won't serve as a boarding pass to Paradise. You see, no one can work his way to heaven. *(Hands notepad back to Dewey.)*

Dewey: *(Defensive.)* If I wouldn't have seen it with my own two eyes, I wouldn't have believed it! And from a lady no less! I can see you're holdin' back my ticket just 'cause I don't talk as smooth as you city slickers.

Agent: It's not that at all. In fact, discrimination is something we avoid at all costs.

Buddy: *(To agent.)* Well, my ol' friend Dewey may be down, but he ain't out yet. I'll betcha he's got somethin' in his suitcase that'll fit the bill!

Dewey: Hey, thanks, Buddy. I almost forgot.

(Dewey opens the suitcase and retrieves the framed diploma. He then proudly thrusts it into the hands of the ticket agent.)

Dewey: You probably don't get the *Sycamore Sentinel* here, but I made the front page the day I got this here diploma in the mail. There aren't too many people who finish the whole course. If that doesn't get me a seat, I don't know what will!

Agent: *(Reading from the diploma.)* "This here diploma certifies that Dewey S. Dewmore has completed the Bible Training Course as prescribed by the I. Tinerant School of Theology and Motel Management. The above graduate is thereby entitled to all the rights and privileges appertaining."

Buddy: *(Leans in close to Dewey.)* You've got 'em, this time, Dewey!

Dewey: *(Confidently, to agent.)* Well, what do you think of that?

Agent: I commend you for your diligence. It's important to be continually learning more about your Creator.

Dewey: I'm in then, right?

Agent: Wrong. *(Hands diploma back.)* It's obvious your mail-order ministerial training has fallen a little short. If you had really understood what you'd been studying, you wouldn't be standing here trying to buy something that's already been paid for. You may be holding a diploma in your hands, Mr. Dewmore, but what you *don't* have is a ticket to heaven.

Dewey: *(Stumped.)* Whew! It looks like getting to heaven is going to be even tougher than my final exam.

Buddy: It sure does appear so. *(Looks down at open suitcase.)* Hey, when did you go out and get yourself a new suit?

Dewey: Buddy, I don't know what ol' Dewey would do without ya. *(Reaches down and pulls choir robe out.)*

Buddy: What do ya mean?

Dewey: This ain't a new suit. This is my Uncle Lester's first preachin' cloak. You've heard me talk about my Uncle Lester's fiery sermons, haven't ya?

Buddy: Sure, but why in the world would ya pack something like *that* in your suitcase?

Dewey: Well, I figured where I'm headed there must be some kind of Heavenly Hall of Fame. If there's anybody's belongin's that should go in a place like that, it's my Uncle Lester's. But now I'm double glad I got it with me. *(Hands cloak to agent.)* Since this here ticket agent isn't too impressed with *what* I know, I'm forced to resort to showin' her *who* I know!

Buddy: Good thinkin', Dewey! One look at that preachin' cloak, and you're as good as on your way!

Dewey: *(To agent.)* I bet you weren't expectin' anything like *this*, were ya?

Agent: You're right about one thing. When it comes to making *this* journey, it *is* important who you know. But not in the way you're thinking.

Buddy: *(Leans over to Dewey.)* Somethin' tells me you're in trouble again, Dewey.

Agent: I'm sure your Uncle Lester is a dedicated individual. But the fact is that no one yet has made it to heaven by hanging on to someone else's coattails. *(Hands the cloak back to Dewey.)*

Dewey: *(Discouraged.)* Well, if that don't beat all. Buddy, it looks like I'm going to have to call this trip off. Since I don't have anything else to give, I reckon the only thing left to do is give up.

Agent: Now you're beginning to get the idea.

Dewey: *(Surprised.)* What're you talkin' about?

Agent: I'm talking about giving up. That's the only way you'll ever arrive at your destination.

Dewey: With all due respect, ma'am, I can't quite get a handle on what you're tellin' me.

Agent: It's really quite simple. But then, sometimes that's what makes it so hard. You see, the only way you can get to heaven is to give up on the idea that you have anything valuable enough to trade for a ticket. Once you've done that, all you do is simply *ask* for one.

Buddy: You mean Dewey here doesn't need any dough?

Agent: Not a penny. It's all part of what we call the "Super-Savior Plan." Of course, a couple of minor restrictions apply. We ask that you begin making plans for your trip as far in advance as possible, and that you stay for at least an eternity.

Dewey: Well, it sounds like the best travel bargain around. I'm sold—or rather, paid for. I'd like a one-way ticket to heaven, please.

Agent: Nothing makes us happier than to fulfill such a request. *(Hands Dewey the ticket.)* Here you are. Enjoy your journey. Just remember one thing. As you travel on, you'll discover that things don't seem quite the same as before. You'll find yourself *doing* things, Mr. Dewmore, for totally different reasons. I'm certain, however, that you'll experience a great deal of joy as you begin viewing life from this new perspective.

(Dewey nods with a slightly confused look on his face. He then begins to tuck his ticket in his pocket.)

Dewey: I'm mighty obliged to you, ma'am.

Agent: I'll be sure and pass your sentiments along to the Individual who's really responsible.

Buddy: Hmmm. Say, Dewey, since you're going to be gone for quite a spell, I was wonderin' if I could have your new fancy fishin' rod.

Dewey: No, you can't.

Buddy: Why not?

Dewey: 'Cause you're comin' with me!

Buddy: *(Surprised.)* What? I can't afford to take a trip to heaven!

Dewey: Buddy, with the deal these folks are puttin' up, you can't afford *not* to!

Buddy: Dewey, you got a point there. *(To agent.)* Ma'am, I'll take one of them prepaid "Super-Savior" tickets to heaven, too!

Agent: Coming right up. *(Hands ticket to Buddy.)* Just follow this hall to the end and turn right. You'll find a sleek new 767 SonShip waiting to take you home.

Dewey: Thanks for everything. I guess we'll be on our way.

(Dewey picks up his suitcase, both then head toward the boarding area. The agent calls out to them again for a final word.)

Agent: Oh, by the way. Why don't you both stop in and say hello to your Pilot? After a short visit, you'll discover where our motto came from.

Dewey: What's that?

Buddy: "Thanks for choosing King's Way Airlines. It's the *(With emphasis.)* only way to fly!"

(Dewey and Buddy smile and exit.)

Thought Starters for "Ticket to Heaven"

1. Jesus says that he is the only way to heaven. What does he mean?
2. Can a person do anything to increase his or her chances of getting to heaven?
3. When does a person know whether or not he or she is going to make it to heaven?
4. You have just been told that you have six months to live. Assuming heaven is your ultimate goal, how would you spend the time you have left?
5. Describe what heaven means to you.

10

What's Les Worth?

Characters

Les Worth, high school student

Mr. Biggs, high school principal

Jim Locker, athletic award recipient

Alberta Eincup, scholarship recipient

Mercedes Benson, most likely to succeed

Janitor

Props

5 chairs, arranged appropriately

Lectern

3 slips of paper with "Self-worth" written on them. These are then taped to Les Worth.

High school jacket (with letters)

Pillow (to make Mr. Biggs fit his name!)

Trophies and/or envelopes (for awards)

Broom for janitor

Self-esteem is hard enough to build up—without others coming along to tear it down.

On more than one occasion, Jesus presented not only a theological truth, but also a psychological principle regarding self-worth when he said we ought to love our neighbor *as ourselves.* (*See* Luke 10:27.) A person must feel good about himself before he can reach out to others.

While it's true that a healthy image of one's self must come from within, each of us tends to become the kind of person we believe others see in us. That places a great deal of responsibility for others' self-worth squarely on *our* shoulders.

In a humorous yet poignant way, "What's Les Worth?" shows how we can unwittingly contribute to the erosion of another's self-concept.

Genesis 1:26, 27; Psalm 8:4, 5; Luke 10:27

The occasion is a high-school awards ceremony. The seniors (all of the students in the skit) are sitting on the gym stage in folding chairs. If more than one row is used, Les should sit on a front seat. The principal sits on the opposite side of the stage.

Mr. Biggs: *(Steps up to lectern.)* And so it gives me great pleasure at this time to announce to you, the student body of Downing High School, *(Looks toward the students sitting on stage.)* this year's senior-class award recipients. Our first presentation is the Quadratic Equation award for academic excellence. This year, our state university is awarding a fifty-thousand dollar scholarship to help pay a portion of the recipient's first-year tuition. And that person is none other than Alberta Eincup!

(The other class members applaud as Alberta walks confidently over to receive her scholarship.)

Congratulations, Alberta.

(Mr. Biggs steps back.)

Alberta: Thank you. Although a lot of hard work has gone into earning this scholarship, I also owe much to my teachers here at Downing High. I share this moment with them. Also, a special thanks to the state university for their willingness to invest in my future. But in retrospect, I realize that it's *(Looks at Les.)* good ol' Les Worth that I am really indebted to. *(Les, surprised, immediately perks up.)* The countless math and chemistry problems he has asked me to help him with over the years has served to reinforce my own education. It is largely because of his scholastic ineptitude that I am able to stand here today.

(A look of embarrassment crosses Les's face. Alberta then steps over and rips a self-worth tag from his clothing. As Les tries to recover, Alberta returns to her seat. Mr. Biggs again steps up to the lectern.)

Mr. Biggs: Our next award is for the Best All-Around Athlete. It should come as no surprise that this year's trophy goes to Downing's baseball, basketball, and football four-time all-stater, Jim Locker!

(The other class members whistle and applaud. Jim steps over to accept the award.)

Jim: Thanks a lot, Mr. Biggs. *(To audience.)* Over the last four years here at Downing, my athletic ability has allowed me to score a lot of points. But there's someone besides myself I owe an awful lot to—*(Looks at Les.)* my classmate, good ol' Les Worth. *(Les now grows even more uncomfortable.)* With a clumsy, uncoordinated guy like him always trying to make the team, it was a whole lot easier for me to look good all these years.

(A shamefaced Les glances around at the others. Jim then walks over to Les and tears off another self-worth tag, which falls to the floor. Jim returns to his seat.)

Mr. Biggs: Thank you for those kind words, Jim. Our final award is one I especially look forward to presenting each year. The person who receives this award is selected on more than the basis of grades alone. It is also based on the recipient's having shown competent relational and vocational skills, along with a high level of motivation. With that criteria in mind, it is my pleasure to announce that the individual voted "Most Likely to Succeed" is Mercedes Benson!

(The class members applaud. Mercedes acts surprised, and then goes over to the lectern to receive her award.)

(Shakes Mercedes' hand.) Mercedes, your drive is an inspiration to us all. *(He steps back.)*

Mercedes: *(Excitedly.)* I just want to say a great big "thanks" to everybody who thought I deserved this award. Of course, no one knows what the future holds. But should I indeed continue to win friends and influence people, it will be in no small part because of the example shown me by good ol' Les Worth. *(She looks quickly at Les, who is by now almost in a daze.)* Socially maladjusted and generally incompetent, Les typifies everything I hope not to become.

(Mercedes now goes over and tears off the remaining self-worth tag. She then finds her seat and sits down for Mr. Biggs' closing remarks.)

Mr. Biggs: Thank you, Mercedes, for showing us that *others* play an important role in determining what we ourselves will eventually become. That brings our annual awards ceremony to a close. I trust we have gleaned insight today that will be of benefit to all. Thank you for your attention.

(All now exit except for Les, who sits looking hurt and depressed. A janitor enters and begins sweeping the floor around Les's feet. He then sees the self-worth tags laying on the floor.)

Janitor: *(With appropriate gentleness.)* Hmmm. It looks like you really got torn to pieces today.

(Les pauses briefly, then quietly responds.)

Les: I'll say. But thanks to this royal rip-off, there is one thing I've finally put together.

Janitor: Yeah? What's that?

Les: Now I know just how much "good ol' Les" *(Slight pause.)* is *worth*.

Thought Starters for "What's Les Worth?"

1. Is there a difference between self-worth and self-centeredness? If so, how does one distinguish between the two?
2. Who are the most influential people in a person's life when it comes to self-worth?
3. Think of someone who has made you feel good about yourself. What was it about him or her that made you feel that way?
4. Undoubtedly, Jesus had an appropriate sense of self-worth. From what we know of his life, what are some possible ingredients that may have helped him form this attitude?
5. What are some specific ways that a person can help boost another's self-esteem?

11

The Day the Mountain Moved

A Simulated Forties'-Style Radio Drama

Characters

Jerome Jenkins, hardware-store owner

Linda Jenkins, his wife

Announcer/Narrator

Bert, hardware-store clerk

Art Thompson, businessman

Harry Williams, businessman

Ben, fire chief

Miss Nichols, customer

Props

Bell (for hardware store entrance)

2 pairs hard-soled shoes (to duplicate walking sound)

A couple of boards (to simulate hardwood floor sound)

A couple of cement blocks (to create the sound of footsteps on pavement)

A scaled-down door in frame.

The thirties and forties are now viewed as the "golden age" of radio. Television had not yet been invented, and men, women, and children alike enjoyed allowing their imaginations to participate in the action and suspense of a well-written script. This skit is a Christian version of the old-time radio show.

Jesus tells us in Matthew 17:14-20 that we could move a mountain if we only had faith the "size" of a mustard seed. But many people fail to understand how such faith works itself out in everyday life. "The Day the Mountain Moved" portrays the way one family exercised their faith, and the mountain-moving experience that resulted.

The setting for the skit is a 1940s' era radio studio. Your viewers play the role of the studio audience. Both music and sound effects are a vital part of the production. The actors and actresses should be dressed in a manner indicative of that time period.

Aside from the announcer's speaking to the studio audience, memorization of lines is unnecessary for this type of performance. The actors/actresses simply share scripts around the microphone. Of course, all participants should be familiar with their respective characters and lines.

See you on the radio!

(The door should have a functioning knob with a strike plate on jamb. This prop will be used for door sound effect.)

Siren-type sound device or train whistle (for noon whistle sound effect)

Telephone, with operable bell (or alarm clock)

Cellophane wrap (to crinkle for fire sound effect)

Packing trunk or metal cabinet (for car door slams)

Plate, silverware

2 microphones (one on stand for actors and actresses, the other for sound effects personnel)

"ON THE AIR" sign (lighted, if possible)

"APPLAUSE" card

Piano

Suggested Scripture

Matthew 7:7-11, 17:14-20; Luke 17:5, 6; James 1:2, 3

The radio drama begins with the announcer/narrator speaking to the studio audience.

Announcer/Narrator: Welcome to the Christian Broadcasting Network's studio *B*. My name is Marshall Roberts. In preparation for the live broadcast that will begin shortly, I would like to take this opportunity to explain the guidelines that need to be followed during tonight's performance. Naturally, we ask that you remain silent at all times except when an audience instruction card marked "APPLAUSE" is raised. *(Raises card to demonstrate.)*

At the actual moment we take to the airwaves you will be alerted by the lighting of the "ON THE AIR" sign. From that time on, we request your considerate cooperation that is such a necessary ingredient in making the broadcast a success.

Thank you, and I hope you enjoy tonight's performance of "The Day the Mountain Moved."

(The actors and actresses enter and take their seats on stage. The sound effects personnel should now be in position. The announcer counts down from five to zero, at which point the "ON THE AIR" sign is lit.)

Announcer/Narrator: "The Good News Radio Theater" is on the air.

(Applause card, theme music.)

Tonight's show is entitled *(Dramatically.)* "The Day the Mountain Moved." Starring in this evening's performance are: *(Reads names.)* And now, "The Day the Mountain Moved."

(Theme music now shifts to complement the script.)

We're told in the Bible that faith the size of a mustard seed can move a mountain. Is it true? While we've never seen anyone literally move a mountain, it's certain that obstacles which have seemed "mountainous" to people have been overcome by believing that with God's help, a positive outcome could be achieved.

The year was 1948, just three years after World War II. Jerome and Linda Jenkins lived in a small town in Iowa, where Jerome ran a hardware store. Although the government categorized them as living a fair margin above the poverty level, the Jenkins still occasionally struggled to make ends meet. This particular evening finds them on the verge of such a time.

(Each actor/actress should step up to the microphone during the last line of the preceding speaker. It is important to turn script pages silently.)

(Music out.)

Sound: Door opens and closes.

Linda: *(From afar.)* Jerome, is that you?

Jerome: *(Tired.)* Yes, dear. I'm sorry to be so late. I would have been home earlier but I had a late browser.

Linda: *(Closer to microphone.)* Well, I'm glad you're home. Did you have a busy day at the hardware store?

Jerome: Unfortunately, no. President Truman may be optimistic for the future of American business, but right now business is still pretty slow at Jenkins' Hardware Store. As much as I hate to say it, Linda, I'm afraid that new washing machine might have to wait.

Linda: Now, Jerome, this old washer may not look like much, but it still does the job. We'll get the new machine when business picks up.

Jerome: Maybe I should start charging everyone who says they're "just looking." *(Chuckles.)* At a nickel a look, I figure we ought to have that new machine by next week!

Linda: Actually, Jerome, I'm a little more concerned about how we're going to pay for Betty's care this month than I am the washing machine.

Jerome: I know how important your sister is to you, Linda. Somehow, with the Lord's help, we'll see to it that Betty is able to stay at the institution and receive the help she needs.

Linda: I guess that's what faith is all about. Right now, though, why don't you sit down and have a bowl of homemade vegetable soup?

Jerome: That sounds mighty good. Things may be a little rough, but I haven't lost my appetite over it yet! Say, why don't you pull up a chair, Linda, and read a few verses from the Bible for our evening devotions? After all, man does not live by soup alone, you know!

Linda: *(Scolding good-naturedly.)* I don't believe that's quite the way Matthew records it, but your idea is still a good one. I'll go and get the Bible.

(Music up and under.)

Announcer/Narrator: Even as Linda read, her thoughts drifted to Betty, her younger sister, who was in a state mental institution about eighty miles away. When Linda and Betty's mother had passed away several months earlier, Jerome and Linda had begun making the monthly payments to the institution. It had always been the intent of Linda's mother to leave her daughter enough money to assist with Betty's care, but most of the money was gone by the time of her death. Nonetheless, Linda and Jerome were committed to making certain that Betty would continue to receive the care she needed. It appeared, however, that fulfilling that task would be more difficult than they had thought.

After a hearty breakfast the following morning, Jerome made his way down to Jenkins' Hardware Store to ready it for another day of business.

(Music out.)

Sound: Door bell, footsteps on wood, sound of tools in use.

Burt: *(From afar.)* Morning, Mr. Jenkins.

Jerome: Hello there, Burt. What brings you into work so early this morning?

Burt: I wanted to get Miss Nichols' new bicycle put together first thing today. You know how she gets if she has to wait.

Jerome: I can't argue with that. I guess I'll just have to start getting up earlier. After all, it makes a boss look bad when his employee gets to work before him. *(Both laugh.)*

Sound: Door bell, two sets of footsteps.

Well, Burt, maybe things are looking up. Here come two customers already. You stay here and finish up the bicycle. I'll go see what these men might need.

Sound: One set footsteps.

Good morning, gentlemen. How can I help you today?

Thompson: We're just looking around.

Jerome: Well, that's the place to start. My name's Jerome Jenkins. If there's anything in particular you need, just holler.

Williams: Now that you mention it, Mr. Jenkins, I do have a question for you. With your store being as small as it is, do you ever have trouble keeping things in stock?

Jerome: Not at all. In fact, if anyone ever needs something special, I just give Jim Benson a call over at Benson Distributing. He can usually get what I need within a couple of days.

Williams: Very interesting. Thank you for the information. You've been most helpful. I think we'll just look around a little more.

Jerome: That's fine. I'll be mixing some paint in the back room if you have any other questions.

(Music up and under.)

Announcer/Narrator: Midday approached and still the quietness of the store had not been broken by the ring of the cash register. Just as the noon whistle signaled lunchtime, Linda walked through the front door of the hardware store.

(Music out.)

Sound: Noon whistle in distance, door bell; footsteps.

Jerome: *(From afar.)* I'll help this customer, Burt. *(Surprised.)* Linda! What brings you here? I was just about to head home for lunch.

Linda: I wanted to get out of the house for a bit, so I thought I'd bring your lunch down to you. But that's not the only reason. I think you should read this. It's a letter along with the bill from Betty's institution.

Sound: Paper being handed over.

Jerome: *(Brief pause.)* This can't possibly be right. This bill is almost twice as much as the previous ones. When we talked to the institution, they told us we'd pay the same amount as your mother had been paying. There must be some mistake.

Linda: I wish that were the case. But it seems that mother was getting certain financial assistance that won't be available to us. It's all explained there in the letter. What are we going to do, Jerome?

Jerome: *(Slightly discouraged.)* I don't know, Linda. But we vowed to provide for your sister's care after your mother died. It would be foolish for me to suggest that it looks like smooth sailing ahead. Still, though, I can't help but believe that the Lord is watching out for us. He knows the problems we're facing. Even though *we* can only see more dark clouds on the horizon, I believe God will somehow see us through.

Linda: Maybe it's to remind us of that fact that He sometimes allows difficult times to come our way.

Sound: Door bell, two sets of footsteps approach.

Well, it looks like you've got some customers to wait on, Mr. Jenkins. I'll see you this evening, dear.

Jerome: Good-bye, Linda.

Sound: One set (Linda's) footsteps fade.

So, gentlemen, since you're back again, I'd guess that you must know what you want.

Williams: We're getting there.

Jerome: I don't believe I've seen you fellas around before. You must be from out of town.

Williams: That's right.

Jerome: If you don't mind my saying so, it seems kind of strange that you two keep looking to look, instead of looking to buy.

Thompson: I suppose it can't hurt to explain a couple of things. My name is Art Thompson and this is my partner, Harry Williams. We're planning a business venture just outside of Waverly. Frankly, we needed to find out what kind of hardware services are currently available here.

Jerome: *(Coolly.)* I see. Just what kind of business do you hope to start?

Williams: We're not at a point where I'd feel comfortable discussing details. Let's just say that our visits to your store have been very helpful.

Jerome: *(Somewhat defensive.)* This store's main goal has always been good service. And I expect that will be true for a long time to come.

Williams: Yes, well, we'd better be moving along. Come on, Art, this day's not getting any younger.

Sound: Two sets of footsteps fade away, door bell sound. Single set of footsteps grows louder, then stops.

Burt: I overheard you talking with those two men, Mr. Jenkins. Do you think we're in for some competition?

Jerome: It could well be, Burt, it could well be.

(Music, mysterious; up, then out.)

Announcer/Narrator: At an opportune time later that evening, Jerome mentioned the afternoon's events to Linda.

Jerome: At first, I didn't suspect anything. But after our conversation, it seemed clear what their real intentions were.

Linda: But Jerome, Waverly is too small to support more than one hardware store.

Jerome: Believe me, I've already thought of that. You know, it's a funny thing. This morning I was positive that God would work things out for us. But now it seems pretty near impossible.

Linda: It doesn't look very promising, does it dear? But this afternoon I came across something I'd like to read to you. It's in the seventeenth chapter of Matthew. It says that if a person has faith even the size of a mustard seed, he can move an entire mountain. As I read that, it occurred to me that the only way our problems can be overcome is by maintaining that kind of faith.

Jerome: Well, the Jenkins' mountain seems to be getting larger every day. One thing's for sure. Our mountain will have to move, because I don't see any way to get over it.

(Music up and under.)

Announcer/Narrator: Linda stayed up for nearly three hours after Jerome had gone to bed that night. With a fire crackling in the fireplace, she sat reading her Bible and prayed earnestly that God would see Jerome and her through their current trials. Feeling confident that she had done all she could, Linda decided a good night's sleep was in order. Just as she neared the staircase, however,

(Music out.)

Sound: Telephone rings.

Linda: Well, of all things! Who would be calling us at this hour of the night?

Sound: Lifting of telephone receiver.

Hello, Jenkins' residence.

(*Music, tense; building underneath.*)

(*Pause, then shocked.*) What? Are you sure? Thank you, Margaret.

Sound: Telephone receiver being replaced, then footsteps running upstairs.

(*Frantically.*) Jerome! Jerome! Wake up!

Jerome: (*Still sleepy.*) Wha . . . what is it, Linda?

Linda: (*Quickly.*) Margaret Phillips just called and said the hardware store is on fire!

(*Music, dramatic "sting" chord, end.*)

Announcer/Narrator: We'll return to "The Day the Mountain Moved" in just a moment. But first, these words.

(*At this point, a "commercial announcement" can be read. Care should be exercised to assure that the advertisement is appropriate, and does not destroy the current mood.*)

And now back to (*Dramatically.*) "The Day the Mountain Moved."

(*Dramatic music comes up, then softens underneath.*)

Jerome and Linda Jenkins, upon hearing the shocking news of a fire at their store, dressed hurriedly and drove down to the scene. Upon arriving, the two rushed up to speak with Ben Martin, the local fire chief.

(*Music out.*)

Sound: two car doors slam shut; two sets of running footsteps (on pavement). Fire may be simulated by crinkling cellophane wrap into the microphone. Activity in background.

Jerome: (*From a distance.*) Ben! Ben!

Ben: Jerome, Linda! I see somebody got in touch with you.

Jerome: (*At microphone now, out of breath.*) When did you get here, Ben?

Linda: How bad is it?

Ben: Now you two just take it easy. Thanks to Mrs. Phillips, I and the other volunteers got here in time. Fortunately, the fire stayed near this backdoor area. Since the problem was here at the rear of the building, I'd venture to guess none of your merchandise got damaged.

Linda: *(Relieved.)* Oh, thank goodness!

Sound: Begin fade of activity.

Jerome: Ben, do you have any idea what might have caused the fire?

Ben: The way I see it, there are a couple of possibilities. A lot of times, in an older building like this, the coating on the wires begins to get brittle. You can pretty well figure out what happens when those same wires get hot. That could be what triggered this little flicker.

Jerome: But you said there were "a couple" of things that might have caused the fire. What's the other?

Ben: *(Pause, then seriously.)* Well, the other possibility is that somebody wanted Jenkins' Hardware Store to close its doors—permanently.

(Music, dramatic, then out.)

Announcer/Narrator: After a long night of doing some temporary repairs, the following morning found the Jenkins discussing their situation over breakfast.

Sound: Silverware, dishes.

Linda: I know it seems suspicious, Jerome. But there's a big difference between a criminal act and coincidence.

Jerome: Well, maybe I have been jumping to conclusions in thinking that the fire was meant to put me out of business.

Linda: Jerome, it's easy at times like this to think that the whole world is against us. But after you went to bed last night, I prayed again that God would bring some good out of our struggles.

Jerome: So that's why you were still up when Mrs. Phillips called last night. Well, there's little doubt that prayer has made a difference for us in the past.

Linda: And I believe it will do the same for us now and in the future.

Jerome: I know you're right. I will have to admit, though, that my faith would be a little bit stronger if there were a few more receipts in the cash box. And speaking of money, I'd better get moving. A store can't do much business if its front doors are locked.

(Music up.)

Announcer/Narrator: Even though Jerome and Linda had discussed the importance of faith, Jerome's thoughts were elsewhere as he drove to work that morning. He knew how important Betty was to Linda. What he didn't know was how they could continue to pay for Betty's care. That, combined with the fire and seeming threat of a rival hardware store coming to town, caused an undue amount of anxiety for Jerome. Such worries, however, would have to temporarily take a back seat to the demands of running the store. Unfortunately, the scene that greeted him did little to lift his spirits.

(Music out.)

Sound: Door bell.

Miss Nichols: *(Upset, in older-sounding voice.)* I don't care what you say, young man. If I want a basket mounted on the front of my bicycle, that's *my* business!

Burt: But Miss Nichols, you don't want to look like some old, er, I mean . . .

Miss Nichols: *(Scolding.)* Now, you listen here, young man—

(Jerome clears his throat loudly.)

Burt: *(Surprised.)* Oh, Mr. Jenkins! I was just telling Miss Nichols that her bicycle would look a little sportier without a basket on the front.

Miss Nichols: Sportier, wortier! It's my dollar bill, and I'll put whatever I feel like on my bicycle!

Burt: But nobody wants a basket . . .

Jerome: *(Interrupting.)* Burt, if Miss Nichols prefers a basket on the front, then she'll have one.

Miss Nichols: Indeed!

Jerome: Please take care of it, Burt. It won't take but a few minutes.

Burt: *(Resignedly.)* All right, Mr. Jenkins.

Sound: Footsteps fade.

Miss Nichols: *(Regaining composure.)* So, Jerome, I had a quick look out back. It appears to me that you were very lucky.

Jerome: Yes, it sure could've been worse. I'd hate to think what might've happened had the flames made it over to the paint cans.

Miss Nichols: Besides the fire, how has business been?

Jerome: You picked one humdinger of a day to ask that question. To be quite honest, things seem to be on a downhill slide right now.

Miss Nichols: I'm sorry to hear that. Do you think things will turn around soon?

Jerome: I'd like to believe so, but a person's faith can only stand up under so much. Linda and I have been praying about the business, but I'm beginning to wonder if the Lord has been listening.

Miss Nichols: Well, you know I'll be glad to help any way I can, Jerome.

Sound: Door bell. Two sets of footsteps walk toward microphone.

Jerome: *(Softly.)* I'm afraid *I* may have been a little *too* helpful to these fellows. I will have to give them credit for their persistence, though.

Miss Nichols: Whatever do you mean?

Jerome: Oh, nothing. Please excuse me. *(Slight pause.)* Well, gentlemen, I see you're back.

Thompson: Yes. But this time we'd like to discuss something specific. It has to do with your hardware store.

Jerome: *(Assertive.)* You can stop right there. I don't know what you have to say to me, but I think you gentlemen should know that, regardless of your plans, I don't intend to be forced out of business. I've spent a lot of years learning what people in this town need, and that's more important to folks than a fancy new sign on the block.

Williams: *(Laughing.)* Whoa, there, Mr. Jenkins! I think there's been a little misunderstanding. Closing down your business is the *last* thing we want you to do. That's why we're here. We've decided that you can be of great service to our new project.

Jerome: What are you talking about?

Thompson: Harry and I are with the City Builders Construction Company out of Davenport. We've been in town finalizing plans for a large housing development just south of Waverly.

Williams: Although it hasn't been officially announced yet, we happen to know that a large manufacturing firm is about to be built over in Cedar Falls. Obviously, that will mean a lot of people moving into the area.

Jerome: Yes, I suppose that's true. But I still don't understand what that has to do with my hardware store.

Thompson: Our experience has shown that a lot of folks prefer to live a little ways away from the sights and sounds of manufacturing. After looking around over the past several months, we've decided that Waverly is just the kind of town many people would like to settle down in.

Williams: All of which gets us back to our original purpose for coming to your store. You see, whenever possible, City Builders prefers to do business on a local basis. After looking your establishment over thoroughly, we're convinced that Jenkins' Hardware Store will be playing a major part in helping to keep this project on schedule.

Miss Nichols: *(Semiwhispering.)* Jerome, if these gentlemen are serious, I'd say things are going to turn around sooner than you were planning on.

Thompson: Oh, I can guarantee you that we're "serious" all right.

Miss Nichols: *(Embarrassed.)* Well, of course I wasn't suggesting. . .

Jerome: *(Interrupting.)* Do you mean you're not planning to start another hardware store here in Waverly?

Williams: *(Laughs.)* Hardly, Mr. Jenkins. As a matter of fact, if things develop as quickly as Art and I expect they will, Jenkins' Hardware Store could soon be doing a little expanding of its own.

Jerome: *(Still amazed.)* I just don't know what to say. But we'll certainly do our best to meet your needs.

Thompson: Harry and I have already asked a few of the local builders how they would rate your service. As a result, we have no reason to doubt your word, Mr. Jenkins. After all, it would be foolish indeed to not have faith in someone who obviously knows his business.

Jerome: *(Pause.)* What did you just say?

Thompson: *(Surprised.)* I said we had no reason to doubt . . .

Jerome: *(Interrupting.)* No, after that.

Thompson: I just said it would be foolhardy not to trust somebody who has earned a reputation for meeting people's needs.

Jerome: *(Thoughtfully.)* Yes, it *would* be foolish not to trust somebody like that, wouldn't it?

Williams: *(After a slight pause.)* Well, I think that's about it for now. If we have any further questions, we'll drop you a line.

Jerome: I can't tell you how grateful I am that you chose Jenkins' Hardware Store to help with your project. If there's anything else we can do, please don't hesitate to let us know.

Thompson: We'll be in touch. Good day, Mr. Jenkins.

Jerome: So long, and thanks again!

Sound: Two sets of footsteps fade away, door bell.

Miss Nichols: Well, Jerome, thanks to the City Builders Construction Company it appears that Jenkins' Hardware Store is back in business.

Jerome: You're right—almost. The future does look brighter, and there is a great deal of thanks to be given. But I believe there's Someone besides City Builders who really deserves the credit.

Miss Nichols: And who might that be?

Jerome: Let's just say he's someone who knows a lot about mustard seeds—and mountains.

(Music up and then out.)

Linda: Oh, Jerome, it all sounds too good to be true!

Jerome: It's true, all right. The way I figure it, the added business ought to bring us enough extra income to be able to pay Betty's expenses each month. Of course, since Ben discovered what caused the fire, some of the money will have to go toward making a few improvements around the store; the first of which will be new wiring!

Linda: Well, thanks to the Lord this will be a day to long remember. Say, that gives me an idea. Hand me the Bible, would you, Jerome?

Jerome: Here you are.

Linda: Now, let me just turn to the Book of Matthew.

Sound: Pages rustling.

Ah, here it is. And now the seventeenth chapter. Hand me that pen, would you, Dear?

Jerome: On one condition—that you be so kind as to enlighten your curious husband as to what you're doing.

Linda: I'm writing today's date in the margin.

Jerome: Well, I'm getting closer. But would you mind telling me why?

Linda: Not at all. It's just a way of helping us to remember a very special event.

Jerome: Oh, what's that?

Linda: The day our mountain moved.

(Music up and under.)

Announcer/ Narrator: "The Day the Mountain Moved" was written for radio by Randall Fishell and Gregory Dunn. The director was *(Insert the appropriate name/s here.)* and producing the drama was/were *(Insert name/s.)* We hope that you have enjoyed "The Good News

Radio Theater's" presentation of "The Day the Mountain Moved." I'm Marshall Roberts. Good night.

(Music out).

**Thought Starters for
"The Day the Mountain Moved"**

1. Is faith something that a person can increase by his or her own effort? Explain why or why not.
2. What is the difference between faith and presumption?
3. If the story had ended differently, and the Jenkins' store had gone under, what would you say to them?
4. Why must a person sometimes continue to ask God to answer a particular prayer?
5. What are some not-too-often thought of Bible incidents where a person or persons demonstrated genuine faith?

12

Something in Common

As Christians, we're called to share ourselves with those around us. In fact, service was really what Jesus' ministry was all about. But sometimes that simple message gets lost in our complex world.

"Something in Common" is a gentle reminder about this all-too-often forgotten aspect of the Christian lifestyle. Join co-hosts Larry Anderson and Terry Sanderson as they reveal just what their four guests share in common.

Characters

*Larry Anderson, news-magazine anchor

*Terry Sanderson, his co-host

Fred Fuller, gas-station owner

Ralph Gunderson, army private

Jamie O'Connor, tennis player

John Doe, Secret Service agent

Mrs. Lou Trent, special guest

Offstage Announcer

*Note: Larry and Terry should be dressed identically. If Terry is played by a female, the outfits should still match in color.

Props

Appropriate attire for each character. (Service-station attendant, army fatigues, tennis outfit, trenchcoat)

2 high stools

A six-foot square free-standing

wooden frame. (A white bedsheet suspended from the ceiling will work as a backdrop if necessary.)

A window "squeegie"

Tennis racket and ball

Pair of sunglasses

Applause card

Suggested Scripture

Psalm 100:2; Matthew 10:42; John 12:26; James 2:14-26

The setting is a television studio.

Offstage Announcer: Welcome to another edition of "Something in Common," the program that explores the fascinating world of similarities. Once again here are your co-hosts, Larry Anderson and Terry Sanderson.

(The applause card is raised, and the two co-hosts enter. They sit on the two stools.)

Larry: Over the past few months, Terry and I have received many suggestions for features on our program. Often such unsolicited proposals result in a dead end. But tonight's program is an exception to that rule.

Terry: Always in search of the more uncommon commonalities of life, we questioned the suggestion submitted by Mrs. Lou Trent of Trenton, New Jersey. A closer look at Mrs. Trent's idea, however, resulted in one of "Something in Common's" most informative episodes ever.

(Fred enters and steps inside the frame, or in front of the sheet, if used.) This is to create the effect of a large-screen studio monitor. As Terry continues speaking, Larry walks over and stands beside Fred.)

Our research took us first to Fred's Fill 'Em Up, located at the corner of Thirty-fifth and Oakton, where Larry spoke with station owner Fred Fuller.

Larry: *(With microphone, to "camera.")* In a business climate where the bottom line is usually given top priority, one wonders how Fred

Fuller's gas station could weather much of an economic storm. Fred's Fill 'Em Up is a "full service" gas station, the last of a dying breed of American pit stops. But Mr. Fuller isn't about to stop doing the kinds of things he sees as important. *(To Fred.)* Fred, the obvious question is, Why do you do it?

Fred: The way I figure it, I can't afford *not* to give my customers full service.

Larry: Could you explain more fully?

Fred: Well, it seems like lately everybody's gettin' into *self* service. But there are a few of us left that still believe providing *full* service is the best way to go.

Larry: Any particular reason?

Fred: The best reason I can think of is that a lot of folks out there just seem to need what we have to offer. So we try to do whatever we can to make the customer's journey a little smoother. Over the long haul, we think it pays off.

Larry: You said "we." Does this mean your employees share your philosophy about service?

Fred: He did, but since Ralph decided to join the army, I'm the only one running the place right now. Whoever I hire next, though, will have to think along the same lines I do on at least one point—giving the customer *full* service.

Larry: Thank you, Fred Fuller.

(Fred exits, and Larry returns to the studio stage.)

Terry: Obviously, sharing "Something in Common" requires that at least one other individual be involved. With that in mind, your "Something in Common" commentators next traveled to Fort Slipshod, Arkansas. Shortly, we located Mr. Fuller's former employee, Private Ralph W. Gunderson.

(Ralph enters from the opposite side of the stage, and steps inside the frame. He is dressed in fatigues and appears tired. Terry then walks over and steps into the picture.)

Larry: After Terry briefly explained the purpose of our visit, Private Gunderson graciously accepted our invitation to appear before the "Something in Common" camera.

Ralph: *(Yawning.)* Excuse me. I had to pull guard duty last night. I'm pretty well bushed.

Terry: You do appear to be rather fatigued. Ralph, from automobile-maintenance man to Private Fourth-Class. What caused this sudden "about face" in your career plans?

Ralph: It happened last Memorial Day. The Fill 'Em Up is open on a lot of holidays, just in case folks might have forgotten to gas up beforehand. Anyway, it was getting dark, and who should pull in but Mr. Sweeney, with a burned-out headlight. Well, Mr. Fuller always encouraged me to take care of those kind of problems for our customers, so I got right on it.

Terry: We've become aware of Mr. Fuller's viewpoint on that subject.

Ralph: As I was working on the headlight, Mr. Sweeney got to talking about the son he'd lost during the war. I could tell he still missed him a lot, because his voice cracked a couple of times during our conversation. Our talk didn't last all that long, but I knew Mr. Sweeney thought his son was the greatest hero this world had ever known. Well, I finished putting the headlamp in, and Mr. Sweeney paid me and pulled out. That's when it happened.

Terry: That's when *what* happened?

Ralph: *(Dramatically.)* I felt called to join the service. As I stood there watching Mr. Sweeney drive away, I suddenly realized that it was because of *his* son that *I* was able to live in freedom. When I thought about that, it didn't seem like too much to ask of me to give something in return. That's why I'm in the service.

Terry: An intriguing line of reasoning.

Ralph: Of course, there is something else I've discovered that makes being in the service rewarding.

Terry: That being?

Ralph: The retirement benefits. They're out of this world.

Terry: *(To the camera.)* Private Ralph W. Gunderson, a man of conviction, and as we shall see, an individual who shares "Something in Common." Larry?

(Ralph salutes and exits offstage. Terry then returns to the stage area.)

Larry: Occasionally, we find that some of our most revealing interviews here on "Something in Common" are the result of sheer coincidence. While taping another edition of this program, something crossed our set that seemed related to our current topic.

Terry: We immediately realized it had come from a nearby recreational facility. We told the cameraman to keep the tape rolling. Here is what resulted.

(The two quickly step into the frame and Terry begins speaking.)

(Midsentence.) . . . in Newport Beach, California, where . . .

(At this juncture, a tennis ball is tossed in front of the two co-hosts. Larry retrieves the ball. Jamie then enters the frame with a tennis racket, searching for the missing object. Terry signals the cameraman to continue taping.)

Larry: *(To Jamie.)* Excuse me, but could you possibly be looking for this? *(Holds out tennis ball.)*

Jamie: *(Embarrassed, takes ball.)* Why, yes, thank you. I guess my backhand still needs a little work. Say, aren't you Larry Anderson of "Something in Common"?

Larry: *(Modestly.)* Well, yes, ma'am, I am. And speaking of that, I wonder if you would mind answering a couple of questions for our viewing audience, Ms. . . .

Jamie: O'Connor, Jamie O'Connor. *(Primps hair.)* No, I guess I don't mind.

Larry: *(With microphone now.)* Ms. O'Connor, just how long have you been involved in this particular sport?

Jamie: Not that long, really. Until recently I was strictly a spectator. But then one day I said to myself, "Jamie, you'd probably enjoy yourself more if you were actually out there playing the game." So I decided to give it a try, and sure enough, I was right!

Larry: So actually being involved was a key ingredient for you.

Jamie: That's right.

Terry: *I'm* curious about something, Ms. O'Connor. In your opinion, is there any one part of the game that's especially important?

Jamie: Definitely.

Larry: What might that be?

Jamie: The serve. If there's one thing I've learned about this sport, it's that a theoretical knowledge of the game just isn't enough. And I've discovered there's no better time to put into practice what I've learned than the moment I shout, "Service!"

Larry: Well, I'm confident that our "Something in Common" viewers have "netted" some sound advice here today. Thank you.

Jamie: I hope I've been able to help.

(Jamie exits. Larry and Terry once again return to the stage area.)

Terry: To the regular viewer of the evening news, the location of our last interview will undoubtedly be familiar. Sixteen-hundred Pennsylvania Avenue is of course the address of the Chief Executive and the First Lady.

(As Terry continues speaking, Larry walks over and enters the frame. He peers around, trying to spot his so-far absent interviewee.)

But it is also home to another individual; someone who, in at least one way, shoulders nearly as much responsibility as the president himself. Our so-far anonymous interviewee agreed to rendezvous with us at a specific location just east of the south lawn.

(John now approaches. He walks secretively, continually glancing around. He is wearing a trenchcoat and sunglasses. As he enters the frame, Larry approaches him.)

Larry: Excuse me, but are you the person who agreed to appear on "Something in Common"?

John: *(Whispering, and looking shiftily around.)* Let's try and keep it down. But, yeah, I'm your man.

Larry: *(Softer now.)* For those who may be unacquainted with the delicacy of your position, would you please tell our audience your name and what it is that you do?

John: *(Continues his eye movement.)* The name's "Doe, John Doe." I'm a member of the Secret Service.

Larry: I've run into that name on occasion, but I never knew who it was until now. I suppose that's only natural, though, considering the nature of your occupation.

John: True. Confidentiality is critical to the success of our organization. Every service we provide is done in secret.

Larry: Hence the name *Secret* Service.

John: That's what it means.

Larry: I can understand the need for secrecy in your line of work. But tell me something. Doesn't it ever bother you that people can't fully appreciate the service you're providing?

John: Not at all. Every Secret Service agent receives extensive training to prepare him for his duties. By the time this training period is over, most agree that fanfare and glitter would only hinder their effectiveness.

Larry: I assume this covertness is encouraged from the very beginning of an agent's term of duty.

John: Absolutely. Our manual states clearly that everyone in our ranks is expected to adhere to this policy. And we always go *(Slight pause.)* by the book.

Larry: Mr. Doe, thank you for taking the time to share with us some of the secrets behind your service.

(John stealthily exits. Larry returns to the stage.)

Terry: Well, Larry, it looks like that all-important moment has arrived.

Larry: Indeed it has, Terry. *(To audience.)* Of course, the moment we're referring to is that which we've set aside to prove that our four interviewees do indeed have "Something in Common."

Terry: But tonight we have a special guest to assist us. Ladies and gentlemen, please welcome the person who first suggested tonight's feature—Mrs. Lou Trent!

(The applause card is raised, and Mrs. Trent enters.)

Mrs. Trent, welcome to "Something In Common." *(Shakes Terry's hand, then Larry's.)*

Mrs. Trent: Thank you, Terry, Larry. It's a thrill to be here.

Larry: Mrs. Trent, we've seen and heard from four different people who, if your assumption turns out to be correct, have more in common than even they themselves may realize. Terry, I noticed an occasional comment during our interviews that seemed especially revealing. What about you?

Terry: There were many, actually, but time allows for us to recall only a few.

(Here, each person steps into the frame as their name is mentioned, and remains there.)

First, Fred Fuller of Fred's Fill 'Em Up suggested the only way he's interested in doing business is by providing his customers full *service*.

Larry: Next, Private Ralph Gunderson told us that it was a feeling of being "called" that led him to join the *service*.

Terry: Our third interview resulted in Jamie O'Connor's emphasizing the fact that victory or defeat is oftentimes determined at the moment she calls out *"Service."*

Larry: And finally, John Doe informed us that "going by the book" is an all-important axiom to members of the Secret *Service*.

Terry: *(Quickly, and more excitedly.)* All of which can only lead us to conclude that the uncommon commonality shared by these four individuals is . . .

(All four individuals respond in unison. Fred holds up a window "squeegie," Ralph salutes, Jamie swings her tennis racket, and John looks cautiously around.)

All: *(Shouting, except for John, who whispers loudly.)* Service!

Larry: Yes, indeed. The single thread that binds this seemingly diverse quartet together is the centrality of service to their lives.

Terry: And that about wraps up this edition of our program. But before we leave, let's find out just a little bit more about our special guest. Mrs. Trent, your letter mentioned that the idea for tonight's program came to you while you were at work. Just where are you employed?

Mrs. Trent: I work for the Trenton Manufacturing Company.

Terry: And what does that company do?

Mrs. Trent: We make a lot of different things, but our mainstay is plastic table *service.*

Larry: With that, we'd like to thank everyone who appeared on tonight's show. Until next time, this is Larry Anderson. . .

Terry: And Terry Sanderson reminding you that, you too, have *(Terry/ Larry in unison.)* "Something in Common."

(The applause card is raised.)

Offstage Announcer: "Something in Common" has been brought to you as a public *service* of this station.

Thought Starters for "Something in Common"

1. What is Christian service? Try defining it, and give a couple of examples.
2. In the Christian's life, which comes first—"inreach" or "outreach"? Is it different for different people? Why?
3. How does serving others bring us closer to Jesus?
4. Why do we sometimes find it difficult to become enthusiastic about serving others?
5. How can a person "serve" another individual who doesn't want service?